Entrepreneur
MAGAZINE'S

Reveals
Hidden
Deductions
That Save
Thousands!

TAXPERTISE
The COMPLETE Book of

and Tax Deductions
for Small Business
the IRS Doesn't Want You to Know

Bonnie Lee, E.A.

EP
Entrepreneur
Press

This book is intended to be a guide to familiarize the reader with tax and business concepts. It is not intended to provide legal or tax advice. At the time this book was written, all information was current. Tax law is subject to constant revision and change. In fact, the answer to almost every tax question is: It depends. I therefore encourage the reader to consult with a tax professional who can discern the best course of action in relation to his or her financial situation.

Editorial Director: Jere L. Calmes
Cover Design: Beth Hansen-Winter
Production and Composition: Eliot House Productions

This publication is designed to provide accurate and authoritative information in regard to the subject matter covered. It is sold with the understanding that the publisher is not engaged in rendering legal, accounting, or other professional services. If legal advice or other expert assistance is required, the services of a competent professional person should be sought.

Multiple forms icon ©Patrick McCall/Shutterstock
Tax form icon ©Rob Wilson/Shutterstock

Library of Congress Cataloging-in-Publication Data
Lee, Bonnie.
    Taxpertise: the complete book of dirty little secrets and tax deductions for small business the IRS doesn't want you to know/by Bonnie Lee.
    p.   cm.
    Includes index.
    ISBN-10: 1-59918-350-1 (alk. paper)
    ISBN-13: 978-1-59918-350-3 (alk. paper)
    1. Small business—Taxation—Law and legislation—United States. I. Title.
KF6491.L44 2009
343.7305'268—dc22   2008055438

Printed in Canada
13 12 11 10 09   10 9 8 7 6 5 4 3 2 1

Dedicated to my mother, for teaching me independence,
resourcefulness, and creativity.
You made me the person I am today.

I love you bigger than the whole wide world.

Contents

PART I
Getting Organized and Tracking for Taxes

PART II

Cozy Business

PART III

Business Deductions

PART IV

Bull and Red Flags

PART VI

We're In Real Trouble Now

PART VII

Appendices

Acknowledgments

I want to thank Katharine Sands of the Sarah Jane Freymann Literary Agency for wanting to hear stories about my day job and planting the seed for the birth of this book. More than that, she watered it, lovingly tended it, and then when it blossomed, she found a home for it. Thanks, Katharine.

To Gretchen Kelley, who believed in the importance of folks acquiring taxpertise and spreading the word. To Stephanie and Bob at KSVY, who gave me a platform to educate listeners and verbally express my views on taxes. To Tami

Casias, Patricia Henley, Carole Kelleher, and Dr. Julie Carlson—my writing "therapy" group—for their wisdom, support, and editorial opinion. Love the candor and honesty—so much more valuable than encouraging platitudes. And I want to express extra gratitude to Carole, who at the final hour offered her eyes and wisdom and spaghetti. My sidekick Amanda Johnson, who took over the workload while I labored on this book and who co-hosts the *Taxpertise* radio show, is like a daughter to me, and I hold her very dear to my heart. To Robert Mathison, E.A., who critiqued the work adding a round of applause.

And of course, I want to extend my appreciation to Jere Calmes at Entrepreneur Press, who liked my voice enough to take a chance on this first-time writer. Also, special thanks to Courtney Thurman, Jillian McTigue, and Leanne Harvey of Entrepreneur Press for their guidance and talent; to Cheryl Kimball for looking at the big picture; and Karen Billipp for her expertise and eagle eye.

Preface

The Clan of the Bean Counters

*A*s I nod off, my mind wanders to thoughts of Silverback. We've wanted each other since we were budding adolescents. I was in love the moment he scooped a handful of red grubs and offered them to me. Silverback is hot. Broad forehead, shining eyes (especially for me), taller and more massive than the others. And smart. He even walks upright most of the time. But Silverback left with the clan chief's sons on a quest for fire and has never returned. Now the stupid and selfish Grong and I have been mates for some time.

I am dozing, leaning into the curve of a splayed branch at the top of a tall tree where I had shaken fruit down to Grong, then eaten my fill. I jerk awake at an unmistakable scent arriving on the late afternoon breeze. Musty musk with overtones of eucalyptus. Alert, I sniff the air and strain my eyes.

"Silverback!" I call to him. He hears me and hurries in our direction, wild with eagerness. I can't wait for him to throttle Grong.

Grong assumes a fighting stance. But Silverback has no fear. He lunges, swinging the thigh bone of a brontosaurus in a threatening arc. Grong screams and scampers away. My heart pounds wildly in my chest.

Silverback smiles up at me. Our eyes meet, all the missed love shining through. I hand him some fruit. He tilts his head and says, "That's a taxable event."

■   ■   ■

"Huh?" I jerk awake and look around. It's 1986 and I'm one of 200 attending a tax seminar. "Silverback" is in a suit at the front of the room. The "thigh bone" is a pointer jabbing at a projection of a diagram with lots of arrows, boxes, and dollar signs.

I shake my head and look around me at all the suits and bald heads and number-two pencils. And I begin to wonder about life and taxes and paperwork. How did this happen? How did we go from a being planet of humanoids with nothing better to do than climb trees and club saber-toothed tigers to being a bunch of nitpicky, paperwork-driven idiots happily adding layer after layer of complexity to what should have been a beautiful and carefree existence?

OK, I understand that's a sweeping statement and there's more to it than that—yadda yadda yadda. But dang! I have just been yanked from an encounter with macho Silverback bad boy. I am not in a good mood.

The speaker says, "You are required to take an IRA distribution by April 1st of the year following the year in which you reach the age of 70½ …"

I lose it. My eyes roll, I groan, and I bang my head rhythmically on the table, repeating the speaker, "The year following the year in which you reach the age of 70½?" What the hell? Why don't they just say you have to take your IRA distribution when you're 70? *Why can't they say that?*

What the hell is with the half? I mean, c'mon, who uses a half after his age? Apparently, the doddering old congressman who made up this law, that's who. I can see him now, wandering around the U.S. Capitol, saying, "I get to sit in the front row. I have seniority. I'm 70½." Sure, pop, have a seat and another Jack Daniels. What the hell.

Once your age hits double digits, the half is history. Am I not right? Nobody winces or thinks twice when you say you're 7½. But people will start wondering about you if you say you're 38½.

I knew right then and there that dealing with tax law was going to be not only a challenge but also a lot more fun than being a Realtor,®which had been my other choice of day job. The tax code is littered with tons of great material for a comedy routine. I could envision it: Do taxes for a few years, then pursue my lifelong ambition of being a stand-up comic.

And the more I delved into the tax code, the more I began to see how subjective tax law is and how much of it is based on facts and circumstances rather than on a cut-and-dried set of rules. Not that the code isn't laced with rules. But hey, it's set up so you can put a spin on it. Wow!

I thought creativity wouldn't be allowed in the tax business. Boy was I wrong. During the next 20-odd years, I felt my creative juices flowing every day.

Recently at a tax conference, the instructor told us, "The answer to every tax question is: 'It depends.'"

The truest words about taxes ever spoken.

Introduction

The first step to financial health is financial consciousness. So get conscious of this: Approximately 43 percent of every dollar you make goes back to the government in taxes. And that's just an average. If you're self-employed, you get to pay extra. And if you make the really big bucks, you could be paying upwards of 50 percent.

That probably ticks you off. Are there legal ways to reduce that percentage? How do you get ahead, you wonder?

Usually by investing. If you read all the latest tomes on the subject, you'll find that creating passive income is the key to financial success. Invest in a home that will not only provide you shelter but will grow in value. Invest in just the right stock and make a killing. Toss some money into CDs for a conservative return. Buy rental real estate. Hey! With no money down! Move your equity into a new business venture. And don't forget to fund your retirement plan.

All of that requires having a few extra bucks lying around. Even if you have the opportunity to jump into real estate with no money down be very careful. You need a deep pocket to keep up in the real estate game. Tenants trash rentals; properties can go vacant for months at a time. You've got to keep paying the mortgage, insurance, and taxes no matter whether someone is paying the rent or not. And if the place gets damaged, you have to shell out for repairs to protect your investment.

Instead of equity buildup you sometimes have to ride out downturns. You saw the economy head south in 2008. No money down is now probably a thing of the past. The economy is sensitive and subject to the domino effect.

Here's my point: You need extra money to get ahead. It takes money to make money. You can create budgets, eliminate your Starbucks habit, and cut corners here and there. Do those new habits stick? Do they really?

Having *taxpertise* is an easier way to create extra disposable income. It's as simple as making an investment of time to understand your tax return so that you may legally take dollars away from the tax man to further your own fortune. There is a way to parlay tax dollars into personal funds that can be invested in anything from real estate to stocks to CDs. Or better yet, you might want to roll the money back into your own business venture.

I will show you how to reroute those tax dollars away from the tax man and make them yours. Imagine having extra money to throw at growth investments or to fund your kids' higher education or even for a well-earned vacation.

Hey, forget the kids' higher education! (Well, for right now anyway.) It's time for your own higher education.

Every day, thousands of people shake off the golden handcuffs and become self-employed. There's not much in our formal educational system that prepares the budding entrepreneur for this challenge. You can study business in college and earn an MBA, but that is theory, not real life.

I feel that the senior year of high school should be devoted to what I call real-life education. Forget about the signing of the Magna Carta in 1215 and the study of Hawthorne's works. I'm not saying those subjects aren't important. Believe me, they are. But bond that into their heads during the first 11 years of schooling. By the time the kids are entering their senior year of high school, they should be turned on to the tools they will need for making career and financial decisions in the years to come.

Seniors should be taught how to balance a checkbook; write a resume; apply and interview for a job; buy a house; fill out a tax return; evaluate, apply for, and maintain good credit; budget and manage finances. These are among dozens of useful subjects that relate to real life.

The entire school day during the senior year should be devoted to these subjects. However, when kids graduate from high school, they know only academia. They have not learned what they need to prepare them for daily living. You have heard the phrases "school of hard knocks" and "paying one's dues." We would probably hear these phrases less if the high school curriculum included a class on hard knocks. And who knows? Since the subject matter would pertain to reality, kids might pay closer attention and enjoy the learning process.

In my experience, college teaches more academia and theory, as if the purpose of college were to teach one how to become a college professor. The closest that I have seen education match practicality has been at the junior and community college level.

I'd like to see a business major program that tossed theory out the window and put your hands to work. There would be a class in office organization. "OK, everyone, you've got a filing cabinet in front of you, set it up for ABC Shoe Repair Company."

And how about a class in shop work flow and procedures? "We're making bathroom cabinets, so figure out where to put the workbenches, the table saw, the drills, and the paint station."

There are lots of opportunities to obtain free advertising that should be passed on to budding entrepreneurs: "Kids, you're ready to open the ice cream store. Write a press release."

And of course, the dreaded but oh-so-necessary numbers game: book-keeping. "Fire up QuickBooks; we're going to enter some data and pull down some financial statements. Then we're going to analyze them. Anyone see why we're losing money here?"

It's rare that these activities happen in school. But imagine how useful they would be and how much easier life would be if the curtains were parted early on.

Over the years, I have seen a number of businesses succeed and, unfortunately, a number of businesses fail. Being along for the ride gave me the opportunity to evaluate what happened, especially to the ones that failed.

In most cases, the owners knew everything about the products or services they offered. They had prior experience when they worked as employees for The Man. I know they were thinking, "What the hell, if he can do it, so can I, right? And I get to keep the profits. Yeah!" Unfortunately, there is more to it than that. Just because you can run the machine does not mean you can run the machine shop.

A small-business owner must act as purchasing agent, salesperson, manager, customer relations liaison, inspector, administrator, and yes, bookkeeper. You may successfully fill many of the roles I have mentioned. However, the first duty most business owners job out is bookkeeping and taxes.

It is imperative to understand where your business stands financially and where it is going. You need to comprehend the importance of the numbers you generate. More importantly, you need to be able to project and know how big a bite Uncle Sam will take, because Uncle Sam will mess with your working capital as much as he can!

Planning is essential. Financial planning is one of the most important areas of your business plan. To produce your widgets, you need X number of dollars. You have it all worked out. You get the money together and go into production. Keeping proper records will allow you to review your progress with accuracy. Did it cost what you anticipated to produce a thousand widgets? Or did it cost more or less? Were there costs above and beyond what was planned for? Is it necessary to raise the price of widgets? Or can the price be safely lowered and generate greater sales volume and greater profits? Did you select the right legal form so you could take advantage of fringe benefits or did you select one that is cumbersome? Are the taxes killing you? In order to make these necessary analyses, an accurate set of records is mandatory. And knowing what the numbers mean and what to anticipate is even more important.

Your financial statements reveal the history of your company; they are the basis of your budget and future projections, and proof of the fulfillment of your business plan goals. You've got to know more than just how much money you've got in the checking account.

You may feel uncomfortable with a pencil in your hand, unless you are using it to sketch a new product model. You do not have time to become a CPA or a tax specialist. All you really need are some organizational skills, procedures, formats, and knowledge of the rules. You need to know how to prepare your work for your accountant so that your accountant can compile your financial statements and tax returns for you at the least expensive fee. You need to understand the significance of the numbers your business generates and you need to know the government's rules. You also need to understand the inner workings of the tax system so you can make sound financial decisions and play the game with intelligence.

And what's the bottom line? The bottom line, of course.

"I'm your Tax Shock Jock.
I'm going to minimize your taxable income,
maximize your deductions, and
dispel your fears about the IRS.
So listen up…"

Getting Organized and Tracking for Taxes

You Too Can Be Organized

. . . Just Don't Follow Bob's Methods

*O*ne of my favorite clients is Bob, an elderly, easygoing, old-school kind of guy. He has a furniture refinishing business and still handwrites all of his invoices. He doesn't cotton to newfangled inventions like cell phones and computers. Bob thinks a web page is a short story about spiders and the internet is a kind of fishing gear. In his shop, under a pile of brochures and dusty paperwork, lies a relic—a turquoise rotary phone. No pressing one for English in Bob's world.

Bob is probably the only remaining individual on the planet who buys 12-column ledger paper. He creates a not-so-electronic spreadsheet of his business expenses. By default, he has 11 main categories. The 12th column is where he lists all of his miscellaneous expenses. When Bob brings in his spreadsheet at tax time, I always recalculate the totals because, well, sometimes Bob forgets to carry his one.

And I usually have to ask, "No bank charges on your business checking account?"

"Oh yeah. I guess you ought to put down a couple of hundred for that." And so it goes; the tax savings from the deductions I uncover always cover my fee.

Are you starting to get the picture? Bob is definitely organized but not *effectively* organized. And it gets worse.

A couple of days before our tax appointment, Bob sits down with a yellow-lined tablet to list and total what he believes are his deductible personal expenses. He produces dozens of pages filled with itemized categories: groceries, utility bills, birthday gifts to friends and relatives, cat food, dog food, parakeet food, and vet bills. Maybe 1 page out of 20 contains a deduction he can legitimately use on his tax return.

And every year, I shake my head and say, "Bob, you can't deduct any of this.

"Look," I continue, tearing out the page with prescriptions and medical bills, "this is it, Bob."

"What about the house payments?" Bob asks.

"See this Form 1098 for mortgage interest? That's the total there. It also shows how much you paid in property taxes. You don't have to write all that down for me." He could have been watching *Gilligan's Island* reruns instead of making all his worthless lists.

Getting started on the right path to taxpertise and prosperity requires changing the way you do things. It doesn't matter if you're a nine-to-fiver working for a W-2, a freelancer, a perma-lancer, an independent contractor, or business owner, you need to have systems in place in order to maximize your tax picture and your finances.

I proceed to give him a list of tax-deductible items he should track, but every year it's the same story. Maybe Bob just doesn't have anything else to do with his time.

I will give you some organizational skills that are so simple to follow you'll wonder why you had any trouble before.

YOUR PERSONAL FILES

First, let's set up your personal files. If you don't have a spot picked out already, select an area in your home where you can comfortably deal with your paperwork.

(Wait a second, I am reading your mind. You're starting to think home office write-off, aren't you? That's not going to work. A space to handle your personal affairs does not qualify. Better check out Chapter 8 before you get carried away.)

Bear with me as I boot-camp you through a few tips and procedures.

Living without a filing cabinet is like living without a closet. Every shirt, dress, and pair of pants you own has a hanger and a spot in your closet, right? You might toss a dress on a chair after a night at the club; you might leave a trail of socks and undies along the path to bed every once in a while. But eventually you pick up; your clothes have a home, a place they will eventually hang. And so it should be with your paperwork.

It's really not that tough. Every file folder in the cabinet will be plainly marked with the contents. Everything from utility bills to birth certificates to bank statements can be kept in orderly fashion.

And no cheating. No setting paperwork next to where it belongs. I have an ex-husband who used to do that, which is one of the many reasons he is now an ex. No setting up a to-be-filed box on top of the file cabinet, because it

TAXPERTISE TIP

File your paperwork immediately. You've got the bank statement in your hand. Open the drawer and slide it into the folder marked "Bank Statements."

will eventually be fatter than the contents of the cabinet itself. As soon as something as dreadful and boring as filing becomes a major project, it will never get done; you will emit loud, groaning noises every time you enter the room and see the to-be-filed stack.

It takes one second to slide open the drawer and stash a paper in the proper file. Put yourself in the habit of moving that paper from your fingertips to its rightful home.

Go ahead and beautify your filing system using color file folders. Perhaps green folders for vendor files, red for tax files, and blue for bills to be paid. It makes filing a lot faster, too.

If you're thinking, "I can't even keep my clothes picked up; how do

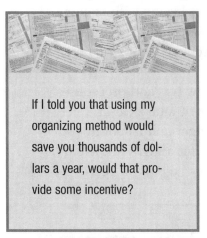

If I told you that using my organizing method would save you thousands of dollars a year, would that provide some incentive?

you expect me to keep track of my paperwork?" my answer is: I understand completely. You are not alone. I have many clients in the same boat, so don't feel embarrassed. After all, we all have our talents as well as our failings. You should accept this as a part of who you are. But because paperwork is inherent to life on this planet, I offer a solution to the problem: Hire a personal assistant, someone who will keep you organized and handle the paperwork for you. You don't even have to employ him full time. In fact, you may need only the services of an organizer. This person will set up systems for you (I describe such a system later in this chapter). Then every six months or so, you may want to hire your organizer to attend to any subsequent messes you have created.

If you don't want to do that, you will need to make an honest attempt to change your habits. Give it a try.

Every year in January, clear the prior year's files to plastic storage boxes and set up files for the current year. Documents for transactions that are not taxable events can be stored or shredded depending on your needs.

STORAGE CONSIDERATIONS

Some files should be classified as permanent and maintained at your fingertips instead of being shredded or going to storage. Others can be stored at the end of each month or year.

Divide a filing cabinet into six sections:

1. *Permanent files.* (Keep these documents handy. Some of them should go in a safe deposit box.)
   - Product warranties
   - Real estate escrow packages for properties with active ownership
   - Home improvements
   - Insurance policies
   - Social Security statements
   - Birth certificates
   - Trust documents

2. *Current finances.*
   - *Bills to be paid.* (Set up separate file folders labeled with date blocks depending upon the frequency of bill paying, e.g., due 1st–15th, 15th–30th.) It's nice to tuck bills to be paid away in a drawer rather than face them day after day as they sit on your desk or your countertop. If they are stashed when received, according to due date, bill paying will be less time-consuming. No sorting through stacks of mail you have already looked at— just grab the current file and pay the bills therein.
   - *Vendor files.* Give each vendor you use regularly a separate file; create one miscellaneous file for one-time vendors. Store receipts for paid bills in these files. Organizing by vendor rather than calendar month makes more sense; if you need to refer to a receipt, it's generally easier to recall the vendor than the date you made the purchase.
   - *Bank statements.* You likely have piles of ATM receipts for everything from grocery stores to gasoline to clothing purchases.

Store these receipts temporarily in the "Bank Statement" file. When the bank statement arrives, match up the receipts to ensure accuracy. After matching, move important receipts to the corresponding vendor file. Keep receipts for any items that are tax-deductible or for which you need to prove purchase (rebates, exchanges, or refunds). Toss out the rest.

- *Tax file for current year.* Throughout the year, toss in any paperwork that is important for the preparation of your income taxes. Some examples include letters from charities thanking you for donations, receipts for tax-deductible transactions, paperwork for retirement plan distributions or contributions, and all those tax documents—W-2s, 1099s, 1098 mortgage interest statements, K-1s, and so on—that arrive in January. Imagine how simple it will be when the day arrives to do your taxes; pull the file and you're halfway there. And if you're ever audited, your backup data is at your fingertips, ready to prove your case.

3. *Prior year tax return files.* Include a copy of the tax return, worksheets, documents from lenders, banks, investment companies, W-2s, 1099s, letters from charitable organizations confirming your donations, receipts for all tax deductions stapled together by category with corresponding adding machine tape confirming the total amount deducted on your tax return. After filing the tax return, store any subsequent correspondence with the IRS and state agency in this file. If you are audited, you simply grab the file and go!

4. *Real estate.*
   - *Escrow papers.* Mark the outside flap with date of purchase or refinance.
   - *Homeowner's insurance policy file.*
   - *Property tax paperwork.*
   - *Home improvements file.* Store receipts and pictures of major improvements, purchase of major appliances, and mechanical systems. When you sell your home, you are allowed to deduct

these costs from your profit before determining if you have a taxable gain. The totals will be at your fingertips when reporting your home sale on your tax return. Even better to have them handy in the event of audit. In fact, when the home is sold, you will move contents, pictures and all, to the tax file for the year you report the sale.

5. *Investments.*
   - Retirement plans
   - Stock transactions, broker file

6. *Other files.* Depending on your individual situation, you will create files to store other documents.

You may want to scan your documents to computer files rather than keep hard copies. If this is the case, please make sure you have adequate disk space and a good back-up system. Maintain your computer folders in the same method outlined above. When arranging your computer files, think of your computer's desktop as a mini filing cabinet.

After your taxes are filed, you may encounter receipts you failed to deduct on your tax return. If the amount is not significant in terms of tax savings, you will probably decide not to amend the tax return. Don't throw away the receipt! Instead, attach a sticky note saying, "not included on tax return," then stash it in the tax file. If you are audited, you will have a bit of ammo to reduce any potential new tax liability.

Your tax return file should be kept in the filing cabinet until the tax liability has been paid off. Then move it to storage. With the tax file, store your bank statements and any other

> At year-end, move receipts from any permanent or vendor files to the tax file if they are the basis of a taxable transaction. Then if you are audited, you need only to pick up your tax file and head for the appointment. If the receipt is important for other than tax purposes, make a copy of it to keep in the tax file and return the receipt to its home file.

documents you may need in the event of an audit. Then if you are audited, you are ready. Just pick up the box and go.

MOVING INTO THE COMPUTER AGE

Now that we've organized your paper trail, I'm going to drag you into the 21st century. Here's a tip to turn your financial life from a living hell to a streamlined process: Track your personal records on QuickBooks, MYOB (Mind Your Own Business), Quicken, or a similar software program.

If you are self-employed you probably have QuickBooks and know your way around the program. Or, if you have QuickBooks but don't know how to use it, go to Intuit's website and find a local ProAdvisor to help you set up and learn the program.

Believe me, the cost will be worthwhile. You will save an inordinate amount of time when it comes to bill paying, balancing your checking account, and compiling your personal data for taxes. And any time your spouse shrieks, "Where the hell does all our money go?" you can fire out a report with every dime allocated, including the inordinate amount he or she spends on season tickets, perfume, beer, classic car parts, clothing, or movie tickets.

QuickBooks allows you to set up multiple companies. There is no extra charge for adding a set of personal books. You can delineate the chart of accounts to include any categories you'd like to track—hair care, pet expenses, vehicle registration fees, chiropractor. You name it, you can add it.

Those accounts that pertain to your tax return can be assigned a "tax line" to ensure that they hit the tax report or are imported to the correct forms and schedules on your tax return. Yes, that's right, you can actually take your tax pro a backup of your QuickBooks data file and if she is using one of the mainstream tax programs, she'll be able to automatically transfer the data to the tax file. Wham! Your taxes can be ready in the blink of an eye.

The same is true if you are using QuickBooks to track your business income and expenses. Rather than print out all of the financial statements and detailed reports, simply take a backup of your QuickBooks file to your accountant. This also gives your tax pro the ability to cruise through your general ledger to look for problems. Then wham! The data is imported and automatically posted to the tax return.

Getting organized can be an invigorating exercise. Life and work will flow more smoothly. You are guaranteed to feel empowered.

Taxpertise Checklist

❑ Buy a filing cabinet!

❑ Get an appointment book (don't forget to write it off). In the following chapters you will discover which tax-related events should be recorded therein. This book will be one of your best friends if you are audited.

❑ Buy one of the bookkeeping software programs, learn how to use it, and *use* it.

❑ If you are simply helpless at paperwork or are a serious procrastinator, hire a professional organizer to get you rolling.

Understanding Your Tax Return

Go Ahead, Try This at Home—No Helmet Required

Kevin and Nancy came to my office requesting help with their tax return. Kevin is a bank manager and Nancy works with autistic children. Both are professionals; both are very intelligent.

"We've always done our own taxes with no problem. But this year, we sold some property and we're not sure how to report it," Kevin said.

The first thing I did was review their three prior years' tax returns. They had used tax preparation software, and at first glance it appeared they had done everything correctly. That's the beauty of these software tax packages. They generate professional, nicely typed tax returns about the length of a novella. One W-2 and you've got a 15-page printout. The software performs red flag checks to ensure you're within the national averages and will be skating under the IRS radar. Charts and graphs inspire confidence and a sense of completion. They virtually promise a complete and accurate tax return.

Even the advertising campaigns show tax professionals with nothing to do, sleeping at their desks because consumers got smart and bought their package, thus elevating themselves to the status of the expert.

How could anything go wrong? It's not like Kevin and Nancy handed me a Form 1040 page torn from the IRS booklet with handwritten pencil scratches, erasure marks tearing through the paper, cross outs, and overwrites. "Ta da! Here's our copy." You take one look at something like that and figure there are probably 50 errors. Look at something generated from tax software and you think, "This has got to be right, it's so damn pretty."

So their 30-page tome looked really good, but when I turned to Schedule A—Itemized Deductions, I immediately spotted a glaring omission. Whoa! They own their house, but no property tax deduction was listed. Okay, so maybe they couldn't afford to make the payment and skipped a year. But when I went through the other returns, the deduction wasn't listed in any of them. Then I noticed another thing. The amount deducted for state income tax paid was equal to the amount withheld on their W-2s. But each year they had a balance due and sent a check with their state income tax return. They failed to deduct that amount as well.

I placed a call to Kevin and discovered that yes, they had paid their property taxes. "What about vehicle registration fees?" I asked, noting the blank box next to that line item as well. "Uh, yeah, we paid those too," Kevin said.

"You always owed about a grand to the state with your tax return. Did you pay those taxes on time?"

"Yeah. We always paid it by the due date. Why?" Then I heard Kevin's wheels turning. "Oh, man. Are you saying we could have deducted all that stuff?"

"Hell, yeah, you can deduct all that stuff, Kevin. You want me to amend these tax returns and get you back, say . . . ," I did a quick mental calculation, "about three grand?"

"Whaaaat? Yeah. Sheesh. I thought the tax software took that all into consideration," Kevin said.

"Well, it would, but you've got to feed it."

Because Kevin and Nancy learned a few new rules, they're now making an extra grand per year. If you understand what elements constitute your tax return, you will:

> Understanding the components of that all-important document you sign on April 15 is key to keeping your money in your pocket.

- ■ know which documents you must have on hand to prepare the tax return and to retain in the event of an audit;
- ■ comprehend how your tax is determined, which is key to understanding and accomplishing preliminary planning, and diverting tax dollars from the tax man back into your own bank account;
- ■ have intelligent and productive conversations with your tax professional during tax planning sessions; and
- ■ be able to determine if your tax professional made errors, made misstatements, or missed valuable deductions. After all, your tax person is burning the midnight oil, ripping through scads of paperwork from hundreds, perhaps thousands, of clients to meet that crushing deadline. Do you think there's a possibility of error?

A LITTLE TAXING EXERCISE

Ready for a little exercise? Pull out your tax return and compare your pages with the entries in the following. This will give you an idea of what documents you need to provide to your tax pro and to keep on hand in the event of an audit. You will also get a good idea of how taxes are structured.

You might even find a missed deduction or two or more and discover that some money is owed to you. If so, file an amended tax return to get a refund! If a line item appears as a bright and shiny object and you're not

CHAPTER OVERVIEW

ADJUSTMENTS (Subtractions from Income)	ITEMIZED DEDUCTIONS (More Subtractions from Income)
1. Self-employed health insurance	1. Medical and dental
2. Educator expenses	2. Taxes—state income tax, property tax, vehicle registration fees, sales tax
3. Retirement plan contributions	3. Mortgage interest, points, PMI payments
4. Contributions to health insurance plans	4. Charitable contributions
5. Student loan interest	5. Employee business expenses
6. Moving expenses	6. Tax preparation fees
7. One-half of self-employment tax	7. Investment broker fees
8. Alimony paid to a former spouse	8. Gambling losses to the extent of winnings
9. Tuition	9. Casualty losses
10. Domestic production activities deduction	10. Adoption fees

CHAPTER OVERVIEW

CREDITS	OTHER TAXES
1. Child and dependent care credit	1. Early distribution from a retirement account
2. Elderly or disabled credit	2. Social Security tax on tips
3. Lifetime learning credit and Hope education credit	3. Household employment taxes
4. Residential energy credit	4. Self-employment tax
5. Savers credit	
6. Foreign tax credit	
7. Child tax credit	

sure if you have a deduction, then go to irs.gov to study the instructions to determine if you qualify for the deduction or credit. If it looks like you need a doctorate in finite mathematics to calculate the amount to enter on the line or a law degree to determine if it even applies to you, then ask a tax pro. These are the things you need to do to become proficient in tax-pertise.

Some of these line items are self-explanatory, so I will not go into a full discussion of them. This overview will give you the gist; you'll have to find all the ifs, ands, and buts in one of the insomnia-curing publications put out by the IRS or by consulting your tax advisor.

OK, all caveats and disclaimers out of the way, let's get on with it.

Form1040, Page 1, Income

The first block lists every type of taxable income you receive. Much of this income is tied to attached forms and schedules. Look at each line item to see the type of income you are expected to report. See Chapter 9 for a discussion of business income and check with your tax pro to determine if there is any other income you receive that may be included as taxable income.

Form 1040, Page 1, Adjustments to Income

Everything listed here will be subtracted from your income to divert tax dollars back to your pocket. Check this area carefully for missed deductions, such as the following:

▪ *Self-employed health insurance.* You may deduct premiums paid only to the extent of self-employment income. If your business suffers a loss for the year or makes a profit that is less than the total you paid in health insurance premiums, you must deduct the remainder on Schedule A–Itemized Deductions. The reason you want to take the deduction on this line is because you enjoy the full amount. On Schedule A, the tax deduction for medical expenses is reduced by 7.5 percent of your adjusted gross income, as you will discover shortly.

■ *Educator expenses.* Teachers usually put out quite a bit of their own personal funds to pay for classroom materials. You can deduct a limited amount here. The remainder can be listed on Schedule A–Itemized Deductions, Employee Business Expenses. You don't get the full deduction if you list it on Schedule A. Employee business expenses is reduced by 2 percent of your adjusted gross income. There is a common misconception that you can take the remainder as a charitable contribution, which isn't subject to reduction. Forget that idea; it's been shot down in the courts.

■ *Contributions to retirement plans.* IRA, Keogh, SEP/IRA

■ *Contributions to qualified health insurance plans.* HSA and MSA

■ *Student loan interest.* Do the worksheet first; this deduction can be limited depending on your income.

■ *Moving expenses.* This applies only to expenses or moving your personal residence. If you moved your business, do not deduct it here. It is appropriate and more cost-effective to deduct your business move on Schedule C. The profit on Schedule C is subject not only to income tax but also to 15.3 percent self-employment tax. Every deduction you can take on Schedule C will benefit you greatly.

■ *One-half of your self-employment tax (Social Security tax).* This amount is deducted here. If you are using a prepackaged software program to prepare your own taxes, the amount will automatically be calculated and entered. This deduction is an equalizer. When you work for wages, your boss pays in half of your Social Security tax and takes a deduction for it. When you work for yourself, you pay both sides because you are the boss and the employee.

■ *Alimony.* That's right! You can deduct court-ordered alimony you pay to your ex. Your ex must show the alimony as income, which is why the form asks for the Social Security number of the recipient. The IRS will match the amount to ensure it collects taxes from your former spouse. You cannot deduct child support. However, check with your tax pro and attorney about the deductibility of a fairly new concept called family support.

- *Tuition deduction.* If you pay tuition to a qualified institution of higher learning, you may deduct the tuition and fees or take a credit against your taxes (see page 2 of Form 1040, Credits). Prepackaged tax preparation software programs will optimize the choice, thus giving you the greatest tax benefit. Otherwise, you'll have to do the worksheets that come with the instructions.
- *Domestic production activities deduction.* This one can be tricky, so you may want to check with your tax pro to make sure you qualify to take this deduction. Generally, if you are self-employed and involved in the fields of engineering, construction, and architecture of real property, computer software, and film among certain other professions, you may qualify for this often overlooked deduction.

After subtracting the total adjustments from the total of your income in part 1, you arrive at your *adjusted gross income*, which carries over to the top of page 2.

Form 1040, Page 2

Luckily, the IRS isn't done whacking away at your income. You get a few more breaks before tax is assessed. The first break is called *exemptions*. A flat amount multiplied by the number of people who depend upon you to clothe and feed them (cats and dogs not included). But check out the instructions for that line. If you make a higher income, you have to fill out a worksheet and calculate a reduced exemption deduction. That's right: If you make the big bucks, the exemption fades away in some cases to zero. This is just one area where the rich pay extra in taxes.

Schedule A—Itemized Deductions

If your deductions don't total the minimum amount to itemize, you will need to take the standard deduction. Check the margin on the Form 1040 for the amount of the standard deduction you receive. It's based on your filing status: single; married, filing separately; married, filing jointly; or qualified widow(er); and head of household.

But if you have enough to itemize, move on to the next page of your tax return, Schedule A, and see what you can deduct.

- *Medical bills*, including:
  - Doctors, dentists, eye doctors, surgeons, specialists
  - Hospital and surgery bills, nursing home care (check the rules)
  - Health insurance and long-term care premiums (amount is limited; check the instructions)
  - Medical mileage for every trip you take for a medical purpose—to the doctor or pharmacy, for example
  - Alternative medical treatments like acupuncture, therapeutic massage, and chiropractor visits (cosmetic surgery is not deductible)
  - Prescriptions (vitamins and other supplements are not deductible)

Your total medical expense gets a haircut; 7.5 percent of your adjusted gross income is subtracted. If your AGI is $100,000, you would have to have more than $7,500 in medical expenses to get any deduction whatsoever. Unless you have a whopping amount of medical bills or a low income, most, if not all, of this deduction disappears.

- *Tax payments*:
  - Sales tax paid on major asset purchases plus the allowance from the tables (see the instructions for this one), or state income tax, whichever is greater
  - All state and local income taxes, including estimated payments, state disability premiums withheld from your paycheck, and payments for current and prior years
  - Personal property taxes (including motor vehicle fees)
  - Real estate taxes (even those paid to a foreign country)—if you purchased a home during the year, don't forget to include the amount of property taxes "paid by buyer" listed on your settlement papers; if you sold a property, look for taxes "paid by seller"

- *Mortgage interest*:
  - Don't be fooled by Form 1098. Just because you have a Form 1098 from the bank doesn't mean you can necessarily deduct

the interest. If the loan proceeds were used to buy the house or make home improvements, then yes, it's deductible. But only to a certain dollar amount. If we're talking a home equity line, the proceeds of which were used to pay off credit cards and take a trip to Hawaii, fuhgedaboutit! That's called personal interest, and it is not deductible. But say you used the loan proceeds to fund your sole proprietorship (Schedule C). By all means, take the deduction on Schedule C. Remember, if you can deduct it on Schedule C, do it. You save 15.3 percent in self-employment tax.

- Note that you can also deduct mortgage interest paid to an individual. Maybe the seller carried back a second or Mom and Dad lent you the money. The loan must be secured by the property in the form of a deed of trust or it won't be deductible.
- Points are 100 percent deductible, but only for the original purchase of your home. If you paid points in a refinancing, amortize them on Form 4562 over the life of the loan—for a 30-year loan, take 1/30th every year. If part of the expense can be allocated to Schedule C, do it.
- You can now deduct PMI, private mortgage insurance premiums.

■ *Charitable contributions*:
- Cash and check
- Noncash (if over $500 in value, fill out Form 8283)
- Volunteer expenses
- Charitable mileage

You'd better have receipts to substantiate charitable contributions. In recent years, the IRS has come down on all fours. There has been a lot of abuse, especially in the area of donated vehicles. Folks were having their rust buckets towed off to some unsuspecting charitable organization and deducting the highest listed *Kelley Blue Book* value. The IRS put a stop to that with a new rule limiting the deduction to the amount paid on the auction block. If the charity keeps the vehicle to use for its nonprofit activity, then you can deduct the fair market value. The charity should provide you with Form 1098-C, which shows the amount you may deduct for donating a motor vehicle.

Political contributions are not tax-deductible. Amounts given to individuals are not tax-deductible. So if you give your McDonald's hamburger to the poor homeless guy going through the trash by the door, it's going to have to be out of the goodness of your heart.

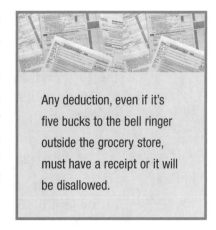

Any deduction, even if it's five bucks to the bell ringer outside the grocery store, must have a receipt or it will be disallowed.

■ *Employee business expenses.*

This includes all unreimbursed job expenses as well as those reimbursed on your W-2. Union dues, uniforms, laundry and cleaning of uniforms, tools, protective gear, subscriptions, professional affiliations, continuing education, resume preparation, job hunting costs, cell phone and computer if required by employer, deductions against hobby income, the remainder of educator expenses not deducted under adjustments to income—the list goes on and on. If you claim any business travel, transportation, meals, or entertainment expense, you must also fill out Form 2106.

A vehicle allowance is included in your W-2 but you must deduct your cost on Schedule A. As you will see, there is a reduction of 2 percent of your income against your total expenses on this line, so you will not receive the full benefit.

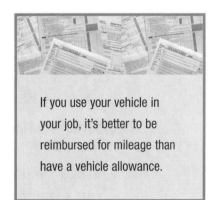

If you use your vehicle in your job, it's better to be reimbursed for mileage than have a vehicle allowance.

■ *Tax preparation, planning, and counseling fees* or purchase of tax software, safe-deposit box fees, account fees charged by an investment broker, legal fees as they pertain to the tax consequences of a divorce (be sure the attorney separates the charge on his bill)

■ *Gambling losses* (to the extent of winnings)

If you win big at a casino, or win a prize in a contest, you will get a 1099 for the value received. You report the income on page 1 of the 1040 and deduct your gambling losses on Schedule A. Here again, it's subject to the 2 percent haircut so you don't get the full tax benefit.

■ *Casualty losses*

A sudden, swift event that results in loss, such as fire, theft, flood, or a car accident is deductible. However, events such as dry rot or termite damage, which occur over an extended period of time, do not qualify. A complete definition and description is provided in IRS publication 547.

■ *Adoption fees*

These are deductible in the year the adoption is finalized.

The total of all itemized deductions from Schedule A is subtracted from your remaining income, then tax is calculated.

But the IRS still isn't done giving you a break. It also wants to bestow credits.

Form 1040, Page 2, Credits

These line items are fairly self-explanatory. They differ from adjustments to income in that they are subtracted from the tax you owe rather than from the income you report. Usually a tax credit is a bigger tax break than a deduction.

■ *Child and dependent care credit.* Calculate and attach Form 2441 if you pay a baby-sitter or child-care service to watch the kids or a disabled dependent while you work.

■ *Elderly or disabled credit.* This applies if you receive taxable disability income.

■ *Education credit.* Lifetime Learning Credit or Hope Education Credit. Claiming an education credit here may not necessarily be better than deducting it as an adjustment to income. Your tax software will optimize the tax benefit, or you can complete the worksheets.

■ *Residential energy credit.* Carrying forward unused credits from a prior year is allowed. You can receive a maximum $500 reduction to your tax liability for installing energy-efficient systems in your home—insulation, energy-efficient windows, doors, and skylights, and so on. Complete and attach Form 5695.

■ *Retirement savings credit.* This credit is fairly new and often overlooked. If you contribute part of your paycheck to your employer's retirement plan, or you fund your IRA or other retirement vehicle, you can receive a reduction in taxes of up to half of what you contributed. It's targeted to low-income households and therefore limited. Calculate your credit on Form 8880.

■ *Foreign tax credit.* If you have mutual funds or investments in a foreign country, you may pay taxes to that country. When you receive a 1099 from your investment broker, you may find a line item for foreign tax withheld. Take the credit for having paid foreign taxes on this line. Check the instructions to see if you must attach Form 1116.

■ *Child tax credit.* You get another tax break if you have kids. Take up to a grand per child off your tax liability. Naturally, this one is also limited, so check the instructions. You may have to attach Form 3901.

Did you notice how many of these credits are limited? All of them. Credits are not given to the wealthy. Some aren't allowed for the middle class either. The education credit is practically a joke. If you have enough income to finance a kid's college education then you probably make too much money to enjoy the credit. Credits pertaining to children are subject to the age of the child.

After totaling and subtracting credits from your income tax liability, you arrive at your net tax figure.

But we're still not done. We're done whacking away at income. Now it's time to pile on extra taxes.

Other Taxes

- *Tax on early retirement distributions*, if you are under age 59½. There are exceptions, so check the instructions or your tax pro, and attach Form 5329.

- *Social Security taxes on tips*. Calculate and attach Form 4137.

- *Household employment taxes*. If you have a maid or nanny, you must calculate the nanny tax.

- *Self-employment tax*. This includes the 15.3 percent that applies to Schedule C income and active partnership income reported on Schedule E.

Notice that other taxes are listed after credits. Credits may reduce your income tax to zero but never to a negative number. The credits listed previously do not apply to other taxes. You have to pay those without regard to unused credits.

Self-employment tax is the number-one cause of tax problems. Taxpayers get a break with exemptions, credits, and itemized deductions to reduce their income tax liability. Yet the self-employment tax stands alone at 15.3 percent of profit from your Schedule C or your partnership with no breaks. The exception is the earned income tax credit given to low-income households. If you qualify for this credit, it can be applied against your self-employment tax liability.

The Final Section

- *Payments*. These include withholdings, estimated tax payments, and credits from a prior year.

- *Earned income tax credit*. The earned income credit is calculated here. If you have low income and children to support, you may qualify to take advantage of this credit. It could mean thousands of dollars back into your pocket. In fact, it's known as a reverse welfare system. Perhaps you paid in no withholding whatsoever. But because you worked and made a small income you are entitled to a big bonus from Uncle Sam up to as much as $7,000.

After subtracting total withholdings, estimated payments, and the earned income tax credit from your total tax liability, you will either have a balance due or enjoy a refund.

Now that you have examined your tax return in great detail, you likely understand how the government determines your tax liability. You may have found some deductions that you should have been taking all along. And your eyes are open to the structure. You are on your way to establishing a strategy that will put wasted tax dollars back into your portfolio.

Taxpertise Checklist

❑ Review your tax return to learn how the tax system is structured and to see if you have errors, misstatements, or omissions. Or ask a tax pro to review the tax returns with you.

❑ Consult a tax pro if you do not understand any elements of your tax return and to review a strategy to maximize your deductions and minimize your taxable income.

Financial Statements

So What's the Plan, Bob?

I received an e-mail recently from a client looking to expand his business. He needed a capital infusion to convert some acreage attached to his home into a nursery. Off to the bank he went. I hoped he would get more than a migraine. I hoped he would get the money he needed. The e-mail went something like this:

Bonnie—
Dammit—these banks are ticking me off!
Can you take a look at this request and translate it into English for me? How am I supposed to know what next year will bring? I've got some basic contracts in place, but will

they renew next summer? How do I provide the projected numbers to you so the bank gets what they want? What's the difference between a P&L and a balance sheet? This sucks . . . or does it? HELP Steve

Here is a version similar to the e-mail request sent to Steve by his banker:

Hi Steve:

Thanks for your 2007 personal tax return and the company P&L through 9/30/08. Can you provide a balance sheet for the business as of 9/30/08 too?

I also need a new personal financial statement (attached).

You have indicated that you will soon send the use of funds for the $50,000 of improvements you would like to conduct on your home property to make it into the nursery. It's my understanding that you want to pay off the first mortgage as well.

If the home appraises anywhere close to the $950,000 you show on the personal statement, this loan would be no problem from a collateral point of view.

So that is where we are as of today. Please send in (1) use of $50,000 improvement funds, (2) new personal financial statement, (3) current and projected P&Ls, (4) balance sheet on business. Thanks.

Tom

As an entrepreneur, it is imperative for you to have a formal set of books. The very first thing to do is set up your books on a computerized accounting program. If you haven't dragged yourself into the 21st century yet, do it now.

As you can see, it's important to know the meaning of the numbers on your financial statements and tax returns. So let me 'splain it to you, Lucy . . . .

FINANCIAL STATEMENTS

You will utilize your accounting data and financial statements to

■ project income tax liabilities;

- know if your business is profitable and, if not, why not;
- provide a basis for performing cost accounting in order to project different profit scenarios;
- provide information to a creditor when applying for a loan; and
- calculate a decent selling price for your business.

Set up your business books on a computer software program such as QuickBooks. If data is posted and the accounts are reconciled, you can press a button and get all of the information you need for any purpose whatsoever, like Steve, for example, who was going to the bank for a loan.

If you are not a numbers person, your accountant or bookkeeper can help you compile and analyze the information you need for any purpose. There are ways for nonmath individuals to wrap their minds around concepts that drive a successful business. I've met business owners who do not consider themselves good at math. But they feel the numbers, translate them to goals, and have the ability to trace the numbers to the sources of problems as well as solutions.

These visual types appreciate the charts and graphs generated by most accounting software packages. Many business owners easily understand their financial picture when they can view it in the form of a color pie chart or a simple bar graph. A picture is indeed worth a thousand words. Visually capturing the essence of your company in this manner may prove beneficial and make it easier to understand an otherwise complex accounting structure.

In today's world, accounting software is available for the non-accountant type. The average businessperson needn't know debits from credits in order to track basic data. Using debits and credits is important at a higher level and can be dealt with by your bookkeeper or accountant. Simple and easy to use, bookkeeping software is much more efficient and effortless than in times past.

You can't take your business seriously until you have formalized an accounting process. Keeping a batch of receipts in a shoebox is not a formal accounting system and it may be one of the factors that will lead the IRS to the conclusion that your business is really a nondeductible hobby.

TAXPERTISE TIP

Another good reason to use accounting software is that the IRS may  actually cut short an audit and settle in your favor if it sees you keep your books in a professional manner. When an audit is cut short, the auditor may not have dug deep enough to find some of those gray-area deductions you were so worried about.

A formalized accounting system will also make your banker sit up and take notice. If you've ever gone to the bank for a business loan, the banker likely requested a current profit and loss statement and a balance sheet. You in turn got these financial statements from your accountant or you fired up QuickBooks and generated the printouts. Hopefully, you didn't overturn your shoebox on the loan officer's desk and ask if you could borrow his calculator.

What Does the Bank Want?

Do you wonder what the banker is looking for when he reviews your financial statements and tax returns? And do you wonder if the financial statements you provide are an accurate reflection of your current situation?

You know that the bank is looking for repayment ability. After all, one of the first lessons we learn in this life is payback's a bitch. And that's exactly the point of view your banker maintains. He's going to throw on his suit and tie and toss around formulas and expressions like "debt-to-income ratio." If after his analysis it looks like payback won't be too much of a bitch, you'll get the loan.

Before you risk this embarrassment, you should be able to review your financial statements to judge the health of your company.

From the personal and business income tax returns, the banker will see your history as well as the complete picture—how profitable your business is, how much your mortgage and property taxes cost you, how many dependents you have, and a listing of other sources of taxable income.

From the current profit and loss, the lender can determine how you're doing this year and compare it with what was declared on prior years' tax returns. So if your business is seasonal and you haven't hit peak season yet, be sure to point this out.

Other Uses for Financial Statements

Aside from bank loans, you need financial statements for purposes of tax liability projection, planning for future expansion, cost accounting, or any other form of financial analysis. Even if you hate numbers, don't be afraid. Ask your accountant or bookkeeper or even a friend or relative who is good at math to sit with you to go over your finances.

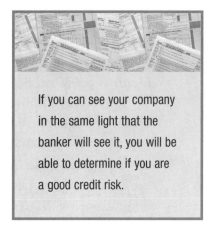

If you can see your company in the same light that the banker will see it, you will be able to determine if you are a good credit risk.

It is imperative that you have a solid understanding of the nuts and bolts behind your business.

THE TWO BASIC FINANCIAL STATEMENTS

There are two basic financial statements: the balance sheet and the profit and loss.

Every transaction you create within your business—whether it's a sales invoice for a customer, a check you are writing, or a journal entry to post depreciation—will end up on the balance sheet and/or the profit and loss.

The detail behind the numbers on the two financial statements is found in the general ledger. Every purchase, every invoice you've billed to a customer, the depreciation you've deducted—it's all in the general ledger. So if any of the numbers look perplexing, go to the backup, to the general ledger. You may discover errors or simply say, "Oh yeah, I forgot about that!" Ask your accountant to correct any errors you find.

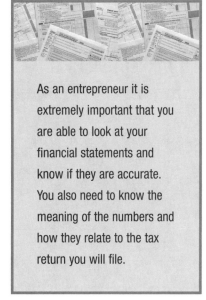

As an entrepreneur it is extremely important that you are able to look at your financial statements and know if they are accurate. You also need to know the meaning of the numbers and how they relate to the tax return you will file.

The Balance Sheet: What Your Business Is Worth

Simply stated, a balance sheet is a statement of your business's worth: a snapshot of your business position on a given day, usually the end of the month or quarter. So if you are pulling down a balance sheet from QuickBooks or another software program, make sure the date in the header line is the last day of the month.

There are three main components of the balance sheet:

1. Assets: what your business owns
2. Liabilities: what your business owes
3. Equity: the net worth of the business; also coincidentally, the difference between assets and liabilities

Assets

Current assets are composed of assets that can be liquidated in a year or less. For example: cash in the bank, petty cash funds, accounts receivable, inventory, and some prepaid expenses.

Prepaid expenses are expenses incurred for a long term, but paid for immediately, such as equipment maintenance agreements spanning one or more years or insurance policies whose coverage extends beyond the current year. If you purchase a liability insurance policy on July 1 with coverage through June 30 of the following year, this cost is considered a prepaid expense and will appear on the balance sheet rather than as an insurance expense on your income statement. Each month, one-twelfth of the amount you paid will be deducted from prepaid insurance and placed on the income statement as an expense for that month.

You can see the result: If you pay $10,000 for a one-year insurance policy on July 1, your income statement for July will not be distorted by the inclusion of that large

TAXPERTISE TIP

Let your accountant or bookkeeper know when you write a check for a prepaid expense by including the coverage dates on your check register.

expense that is truly an expense to be spread over a one-year period. Your profit margin will be higher on the income statement. Your net worth will be higher on the balance sheet because the prepaid expense is an asset. And you will be in compliance with the IRS, who requires that prepaid expenses be allocated in this manner.

Fixed assets are capital items that have a life of more than one year, for example: an automobile used in the business, machinery and equipment, office furniture, leasehold improvements. Long-term assets might also include notes receivable with repayment periods of longer than one year.

Goodwill and covenant-not-to-compete are intangible assets—unlike your computer or your desk, you can't see them. You cannot create values for these and place them on the balance sheet if you started the business on your own. You can show these items only if they were part of the price of a business you purchased. Some day you may sell your business. When you do, you may assign a value to goodwill and covenant-not-to-compete as part of the sale price of the business.

> ## TAXPERTISE TIP
>
> If you purchase a business, it is advantageous to allocate as much as possible toward tangible fixed assets because the write-off on your taxes occurs more rapidly—5 years for equipment and 7 years for furniture and fixtures versus 15 years for intangibles.

Liabilities

Liabilities can be short term (payable in one year or less) or long term (payable in more than one year). Short-term liabilities may include accounts payable, payroll taxes payable, sales taxes payable, customer deposits on work in process, or security deposits made to your business. Long-term liabilities, such as vehicle loans and mortgages, have loan terms of more than one year.

Most of the errors I encounter on a balance sheet are within the liability accounts. More often than not a loan payment is posted completely to the liability account without regard to separating out interest, which is an expense and belongs on the profit and loss rather than the balance sheet. Or vice versa: The entire payment is posted to interest expense, which is fine if it's an interest-only loan. But if the entire payment is posted to the liability account, you may lose a valuable tax deduction.

Look at the liability accounts. Credit cards, vehicle loans, lines of credit, and other business loans should be listed here. Pull out the most recent statements from the lender or credit card company and compare the balances owing with the numbers reflected on the balance sheet. If you spot errors or inconsistencies, ask your accountant or bookkeeper to correct them. I often discover thousands of dollars in lost interest and credit card charges because these expenses are not properly posted to the books—or are not posted at all!

Inexperienced bookkeepers do not understand the balance sheet and often make errors that are reflected in the various balance sheet accounts. All credit card or other loan balances should be reconciled every month in the same way one would balance the checkbook.

Equity

Equity is the difference between liabilities and assets. It's what your business is worth. The account listings under equity vary depending upon your legal form.

Sole Proprietor/Partnerships. If your legal form is sole proprietor or partnership, equity is the difference between assets and liabilities. Here's where the concept of balance comes into play, because equity is also a combination of amounts (from day one forward) that you paid in and drew out combined with the annual profit or loss. Note how these activities are summarized on the balance sheet:

Beginning Capital + Contributions − Draws + Current Year Profit or Loss = Equity

And if the books are prepared properly, it just happens to balance with the equation:

Assets − Liabilities = Equity

An owner contribution is the amount of money and the value of personal property you put into the business from your personal holdings. If you deposit $500 from your personal savings account into your business checking account, you need to identify this separately from sales so your accountant will not mistake it for taxable income. A contribution from your personal funds is not taxable; therefore, it will be classified as a contribution under equity. Contributions also include the value of any personal property you contribute to the business (furniture, equipment, etc.).

An owner withdrawal is the amount of money or goods you take out of the business for personal use.

Fiscal-year earnings are the bottom line from your year-to-date income statement. A profit increases your net worth. A loss decreases your net worth.

At year-end your owner contribution, owner withdrawal, and fiscal-year earnings accounts are summarized into one line item and carried forward to the next year to the account titled "Owner's Capital." For example, in your first year of business, you deposited from savings a total of $10,000 for the year, and you wrote yourself draw checks totaling $5,000. Your income statement at the end of the year reflected a profit of $7,000. Your beginning net worth going into the next year of business was increased by $12,000: ($0 + $10,000 (contribution) − $5,000 (draws) + $7,000 (profit) = $12,000 (ending net worth).

Corporation. If your legal form is corporate, equity involves stock, paid-in capital, current year profit or loss, dividends paid, and retained earnings.

Each shareholder in the company purchases shares. That value is reflected as a separate line item titled "Stock" under equity on the balance sheet.

Paid-in capital is the value of personal property or monies paid in to the corporation that is not otherwise classified as a loan or as an exchange for stock. If paid in by the shareholders of the corporation, it is not taxable income to the corporation. If paid in by other than shareholders, it may be considered taxable income. Review these transactions with your tax pro.

Current-year profit or loss is the bottom line reflected on the year-to-date income statement.

Retained earnings are the corporation's prior years' accumulated earnings. At the end of the year, fiscal-year earnings (profit or loss) and dividends paid are combined with retained earnings, increasing or decreasing the net worth of the corporation.

Because the balance sheet requires advanced knowledge to set up and maintain with integrity, it is important to have a professional help you set it up and review it with you occasionally.

Profit and Loss Statement: How Much Your Business Earns

For any given period of time, the profit and loss statement shows sales less the total spent on business expenses. The resulting profit or loss is the amount left over for the owners to enjoy and reinvest into the business or whine about and deduct from their other income on their individual tax returns. Owners of a C corporation can whine all day but they must carry forward losses to the subsequent year's corporate income tax return.

The profit and loss statement is generated at year-end and given to your tax pro to determine your income tax liability. The numbers are reviewed and copied onto your tax return.

Notice that the business expenses listed on the profit and loss do not include owner draws, which, as we discovered earlier is a balance sheet item. If your tax bill is based on the numbers from the profit and loss, then you can correctly assume that the money you draw from the business is not part of the equation. Many sole proprietors believe that they are taxed on the total cash they take from the business every year. Nowhere on the Schedule C is there a line item asking the total of owner draws.

The first line item on the income statement is sales. You may wish to break out sales by product or service type. That way you know how much is coming in from each source and what products need more promotion or possibly abandonment. A service business like mine may break out sales to bookkeeping, payroll, tax preparation, and so on. A retail clothing store may want to break out sales to lingerie, women's apparel, men's apparel, shoes, etc.

Cost of goods sold is composed of expenses that relate to the sale of your product or service. In a retail business, this includes the cost of the inventory sold during the accounting period and freight paid on delivery from the distributor or wholesaler. For example: Sales are $6,000. You double the cost of your product when you sell it. Therefore, cost of goods sold should be $3,000. If you sell product, make sure your cost of goods sold looks accurate.

Bear in mind that cost of goods sold is just that—cost of goods sold. It doesn't represent the cost of all products purchased or created. You list only the cost of the products that you actually sold during the month on the profit and loss statement. When you initially buy products, post the purchases to inventory on the balance sheet. It's an asset until you sell it. Then it's just gone. And that's when the IRS lets you deduct it.

Each month the inventory account is adjusted and the cost of merchandise sold during the month is moved from inventory to cost of goods sold. Sometimes bookkeepers make the error of posting all purchases to cost of goods sold. Sometimes they post the purchases properly to inventory but do not move the cost of the sold merchandise to the profit and loss statement. Either error will skew your financial picture dramatically and possibly mess up your tax return.

In manufacturing, cost of goods sold includes the cost of materials used in the creation of the product, production, labor, freight in, and subcontracting of any phases of production. Here again, all purchases are posted to inventory and an accounting adjustment is made from inventory to cost of goods sold to reflect the cost of merchandise sold during the month.

TAXPERTISE TIP

If you are the owner-operator of a corporate legal entity, then separate your payroll from that of your employees and list it under "Officer Salaries" on the profit and loss. This will make it easy on your tax pro who must list it as a separate line item on the corporate income tax return.

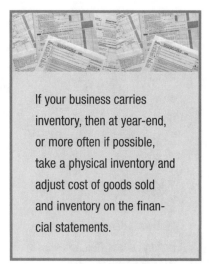

If your business carries inventory, then at year-end, or more often if possible, take a physical inventory and adjust cost of goods sold and inventory on the financial statements.

For the construction industry, cost of goods sold includes materials, supplies, permits, production labor, and subcontractor expense.

In a service industry, cost of goods sold includes the cost of direct labor and subcontractor labor involved in providing services that you sell to your customers. This is a lot easier to deal with because you simply post your labor expenses directly to cost of goods sold. No worries about adjustments to inventory.

Direct expenses include sales expenses like advertising, commissions, vehicle expenses, and salaries and wages to employees who are not in an administrative capacity or are not listed under direct labor. For example: Your employee who installs the product you sell may be listed as direct labor under cost of goods sold. But the high school student you hire to sweep the shop and clean the restrooms and the receptionist should be listed under "Salaries and Wages" as a direct expense rather than cost of goods sold simply because they do not create your product or service. Insurance, rent, utilities, telephone, and shop supplies are also direct expenses.

General and administrative expenses include your office salaries, bank charges, legal and professional fees, travel, meals and entertainment, dues and publications, professional development (cost of education), postage, and office supplies. If your legal form is corporate, officer salaries fall into this category. If the officer is also a production worker, allocate the appropriate percentage of his or her salary to "Cost of Goods Sold–Labor."

Because entertainment and meals are only 50 percent deductible, separate them from travel, which is 100 percent deductible. Providing meals for employees during office hours is 100 percent deductible. Therefore, set up a category for 100 percent meals to distin-

Tax planning is an essential part of doing business.

guish it from 50 percent-deductible meals. That little tip should put a few extra tax dollars back into your pocket.

The bottom line is your net profit. This is the number that becomes the basis of your taxable income. When the tax return is prepared this number may be adjusted downward to include depreciation. There may be other factors that will change the number. For example, adding to profit the 50 percent portion of nondeductible meals expense.

Most accounting programs provide the ability to pull a comparative profit and loss statement to see how this year looks compared with last year. If your profit is substantially different, and you suspect the trend will continue through the end of the year, you may want to consult with your tax pro for some tax planning sessions. See Figure 3.1 for a sample balance sheet and profit and loss statements.

TAXPERTISE

Provide your tax professional with copies of your profit and loss, comparative profit and loss, balance sheet, and general ledger at midyear and obtain an analysis of your potential income tax liabilities.

A MATH LESSON

Brace yourself. We are now going to do some math. It will be a little like those high school questions: If a train leaves the station in Chicago at 2 P.M. traveling at 50 mph and another train leaves Detroit at 4 P.M. traveling at 65 mph and the distance between the two points is 479 miles, what is the engineer's name?

No, it won't be that strange; we just need to do a few basic mathematical calculations highlighting the four basic math operations: division, multiplication, addition, and subtraction.

Print out a profit and loss as of the last day of last month. Prorate your profit to year-end. For example, if the profit and loss is dated May 31, divide the profit by 5, then multiply it by 12 to come up with a projected profit for the year. This is the most simplistic and straightforward approach. After arriving at the projected year-end profit, you may wish

Figure 3.1 *Sample Balance Sheet and Profit and Loss Statement*

11:47 AM
10/01/08
Accrual Basis

Suze's Sole Proprietor Department Store
Balance Sheet
As of September 30, 2008

	Sep 30, 08
ASSETS	
Current Assets	
Checking/Savings	
My Bank Checking Account	4,049.47
My Bank Savings Account	5,398.00
Cash on Hand	100.00
Cash in Safe	300.00
Total Checking/Savings	9,847.47
Other Current Assets	
Inventory	49,135.39
Total Other Current Assets	49,135.39
Total Current Assets	58,982.86
Fixed Assets	
Leasehold Improvements	26,716.60
Furniture and Fixtures	9,031.53
Machinery and Equipment	4,382.01
Startup Expenses	9,347.80
Total Fixed Assets	49,477.94
Other Assets	
Prepaid Rent Deposits	5,622.00
Total Other Assets	5,622.00
TOTAL ASSETS	**114,082.80**
LIABILITIES & EQUITY	
Liabilities	
Current Liabilities	
Credit Cards	
My Business Credit Card	222.43
Total Credit Cards	222.43
Other Current Liabilities	
My Bank Credit Line	7,502.27
Payroll Tax Liabilities	273.68
Sales Tax Payable	1,380.64
Total Other Current Liabilities	9,156.59
Total Current Liabilities	9,379.02
Long Term Liabilities	
My Bank Business Loan	13,500.00
Total Long Term Liabilities	13,500.00
Total Liabilities	22,879.02
Equity	
Owner's Capital	
Net Worth	87,551.72
Draws	
Owner Donations	-350.00
Owner Health Insurance	-650.70
Draws - Other	-14,919.89
Total Draws	-15,920.59
Investments	3,807.21
Total Owner's Capital	75,438.34
Net Income	15,765.44
Total Equity	91,203.78
TOTAL LIABILITIES & EQUITY	**114,082.80**

Figure 3.1 *Sample Balance Sheet and Profit and Loss Statement,* continued

1:00 PM
10/01/08
Accrual Basis

Suze's Sole Proprietor Department Store
Profit & Loss
January through September 2008

	Jan - Sep 08	% of Income
Ordinary Income/Expense		
Income		
Sales		
Book Sales	9,930.10	19.5%
Candy Sales	10,358.45	20.3%
Collectibles	17,090.80	33.5%
Music Sales	13,724.65	26.9%
Shipping & Handling	28.15	0.1%
Total Sales	51,132.15	100.3%
Returns and Allowances	-153.00	-0.3%
Total Income	50,979.15	100.0%
Cost of Goods Sold		
Cost of Goods Sold		
Product	23,304.91	45.7%
Donated Inventory-FMV	675.00	1.3%
Shipping Expense	14.95	0.0%
Total Cost of Goods Sold	23,994.86	47.1%
Total COGS	23,994.86	47.1%
Gross Profit	26,984.29	52.9%
Expense		
Advertising & Promotion	835.96	1.6%
Bank Service Charges	16.50	0.0%
Credit Card Processing Fees	764.68	1.5%
Display Merchandise NFS	126.43	0.2%
Janitorial	144.00	0.3%
Office Supplies	69.38	0.1%
Payroll Expenses		
Wages Expense	1,334.80	2.6%
Payroll Tax Expense	167.30	0.3%
Employee Health Insurance	125.00	0.2%
Total Payroll Expenses	1,627.10	3.2%
Postage and Delivery	70.63	0.1%
Rent	5,561.50	10.9%
Repairs	647.42	1.3%
Security	114.00	0.2%
Shop Supplies	321.12	0.6%
Telephone	299.56	0.6%
Travel & Ent		
Employee Meals-100%	48.00	0.1%
Meals & Entertainment	19.69	0.0%
Total Travel & Ent	67.69	0.1%
Utilities	559.70	1.1%
Total Expense	11,225.67	22.0%
Net Ordinary Income	15,758.62	30.9%
Other Income/Expense		
Other Income		
Interest Income	6.82	0.0%
Total Other Income	6.82	0.0%
Net Other Income	6.82	0.0%
Net Income	**15,765.44**	**30.9%**

to make further adjustments. Perhaps you will subtract any additional expenses that you anticipate between now and December 31. Or add an increased income stream in December around Christmas. Or subtract an expected downturn in sales.

Example: May 31 profit is $50,000. Divided by 5 = $10,000, times 12 = $120,000 profit for the year. During the holiday season sales usually increase $50,000, less cost of goods sold, $25,000, and less additional wages paid for the holiday season, resulting in a $10,000 net income of $15,000. Anticipated profit is therefore $135,000.

Finally, subtract depreciation. If your taxes were prepared professionally the prior year, you may find a current-year depreciation schedule with a copy of the tax return. You can also subtract depreciation and Section 179 expense of any assets purchased this year—furniture, fixtures, equipment, leasehold improvements, and vehicles. You might need a little help from your tax pro to determine these amounts.

After subtracting depreciation from your profit, multiply the result by 15.3 percent. This will give you an idea of what the self-employment tax will be. This works if you are a sole proprietor or a partner in a partnership or an LLC taxed as a partnership. If you have a subchapter S corporation you may skip this step because profit from a S corporation is not subject to self-employment tax. (All of these various forms of business entities are described in Chapter 5.)

To the self-employment tax add your anticipated income tax liability, then compare the total with the total of your federal estimated tax payments.

You may need to adjust your estimated tax payments to make sure you are prepaying your tax liability and don't end up with either a huge bill or a huge refund next April 15. Nothing worse than prepaying more than you have to or getting sideswiped by a bill bigger than you anticipated.

If your eyes are glazed over and you still don't know the engineer's name, then submit your financial statements to your tax pro to help you with these projections.

That wasn't so bad, now was it? So what's your plan, Bob?

Taxpertise Checklist

❏ Review the balance sheet for accuracy.

❏ Print out a pie chart to analyze income and expenses.

❏ Print out a comparative profit and loss to see if profit varies from last year.

❏ At midyear, take financial statements to a tax pro for a tax planning session and to review estimated tax payments.

❏ If you are scared of math, get over it! You're an entrepreneur. You're in the big leagues now.

Estimated Tax Payments

Or How the IRS Takes the Fun Out of Self-Employment

*C*assandra came to my office one day with a brilliant business idea. Her capital was limited but she knew the business would take off and she'd quickly recoup her investment. We worked out the business plan and Cassandra went to it. I had a lot of confidence in her. I think she once sold swampland to Donald Trump. Or was it a beach house in Kansas? Anyway, no one could resist her charm when she went into selling mode.

After six months I compiled her books, then I met with her. "Hey, you're right, you're showing one hell of a profit."

Cassandra grinned. "Yeah, I know. Come outside and look."

We stepped out to the parking lot. "Ta da!" Cassandra waved her hand at a brand-new silver Mercedes convertible.

I said, "Oh, I know you look good in that."

Cassandra angled in behind the wheel. "Get in, get in," she said. "You have got to check out the sound system. I upgraded."

Once we got back to business, I informed Cassandra that it was time to make some estimated tax payments. For the first time that morning, she scowled. "Oh, you're no fun at all. How much do I have to pay?"

When I told her, she gasped. "Are you sure? Maybe you made a mistake."

"Girl, look at your new ride. You know I didn't make a mistake."

"Well, I need to put the money back into the business. I can't pay that right now."

"If you don't pay it now, and you keep going at this clip, you'll owe twice as much come April 15."

"I'll deal with it then." Cassandra huffed out of the office and found herself a new accountant.

Two years later she came back. "I owe all this money to the IRS plus penalties and interest. My accountant doesn't like dealing with them and I'm getting kind of scared. Can you help me clean up this mess?"

"All right, Cassandra. Thing is, you've got to start making estimated tax payments. Will you do that?"

Cassandra's lower lip turned out in a petulant frown. "Okay, fine."

Once your business makes a profit, you will owe taxes. I hate to tell you the bad news, but the taxes you will owe will be much more than you might think. They will be more than what your employer withheld on your paycheck before you started the business. And you thought that was bad!

Here's why: When you work as an employee, the withholdings on your paycheck include the following:

■ Federal income tax

- Social Security and Medicare tax
- State income tax (if you live in a state that charges it)
- State disability tax (again, dependent on your state's regulations)
- Local income tax (if you live in a city that charges it)

When you receive your net pay, you become accustomed to the reduced amount from what was advertised as your big fat salary. The withheld taxes become transparent. Pretty soon you don't even notice the tax bite.

Then one day you become self-employed as a sole proprietor or a partner in a partnership. You don't have that paycheck anymore. You just dip into the business checking account when you need money. And during that first year or two of business, there might not be much money to yank out of there.

When you file your tax return with your first big fat profit of ten grand—whoopee—you find that you owe about $1,500 in federal income taxes. With no withholding in place the taxes are no longer transparent. And you're like, "*What*? How the hell can anybody even live on ten grand much less pay taxes on it?" It's enough to make you want to go to DC and picket the White House. I mean, you would, if you could afford the trip, right?

Why are taxes so high if you're self-employed? What do these taxes represent? Well, here's the deal. When you're working for The Man, your employer matches the Social Security and Medicare that's withheld from your paycheck. The amount withheld totals 7.65 percent of your gross pay. So on every ten grand you make, you lose $765 to the Social Security system. Your employer matches that amount; he kicks in $765 on your behalf as well. But now that you're self-employed, guess what? You are the boss as well as the employee. See where I'm going with this? Yep, you get to kick in both sides to the Social Security system.

You pay two taxes on your Form 1040 when you are a sole proprietor or a partner. Regular income tax and self-employment tax (Social Security and Medicare tax).

TAXPERTISE TIP

If the due date falls on a weekend or a federally recognized holiday, then the due date defaults to the next business day. So if January 15 is on a Saturday, your payment must be postmarked by Monday the 17th to be considered paid on time.

Do you see what happened? The amount owed on the tax return with the ten grand profit is all self-employment (Social Security) tax. Your personal exemption(s) and standard or itemized deductions likely wiped out the profit. You owed nothing or very little in income taxes. The big-ticket item creating the tax liability was the self-employment tax.

That can get pretty expensive once you start making the big bucks. As you can see, it doesn't really matter what financial level you are at; progressively, it will be expensive. Imagine the liability when your income begins to exceed the amount of your personal exemption(s) and standard or itemized deductions. You will owe regular income tax as well as the self-employment tax.

When it comes to taxes, we're on a pay-as-you-go system. The IRS, in its infinite wisdom, realizes that if one is self-employed, it's best for her to pay her taxes quarterly to reduce the year-end hit. The IRS doesn't want you running scared like Cassandra did for a couple of years. You therefore must prepay according to what you believe you will owe for the year.

You make the payments four times a year. The due dates are

■ Q1: April 15,
■ Q2: June 15,
■ Q3: September 15, and
■ Q4: January 15.

There are specific rules that pertain to paying your estimated tax payments. You should discuss the rules with your tax pro or visit the IRS website at irs.gov and look for instructions for Form 1040-ES. The rules are riddled with caveats and exceptions and are often subject to change. Pretty much, the main rule is to prepay the total tax liability (before payments and withholdings) listed on your tax return the year before. If you make more than $150,000 per year, you must prepay 110 percent of the prior year's liability.

Your tax pro will set you up with estimate vouchers and instructions. Or you can download the forms from the IRS website and calculate the payments yourself. The IRS provides a worksheet to calculate the amount you should prepay.

What if in the prior year you owed only $1,500 on your $10,000 profit but now your business has taken off and profits are skyrocketing? If so, you should increase the amount of your estimates before you spend all that money and end up in tax trouble.

And what if business has plummeted? That's easy. You forgo paying the estimate. You probably can't afford to pay it anyway. But unless you're showing a huge loss, make sure you have paid in something.

If you don't pay or you underpay an estimated tax voucher, you will not hear anything from the IRS. It won't know until next year when you file your tax return whether or not you are in good standing. Your tax liability for the current year is not revealed until the IRS

TAXPERTISE TIP

Midyear, provide your tax pro with a current profit and loss statement to review and adjust your estimated tax payments accordingly.

processes your tax return long after the year is over. It is at that point that it will decide if you have made payments on time and in sufficient amounts to cover your liability. If you haven't, the IRS will calculate penalties and interest and send you a bill.

You can escape underpayment penalties if you owe less than $1,000 (according to current regulations; check with your tax pro) or you had no tax liability the previous year.

If you receive a notice from the IRS regarding underpayment of estimated taxes or you discover a penalty at the bottom of page 2 of your 1040, fill in Form 2210, Underpayment of Estimated Tax by Individuals, to see if you are really deserving of the penalty. Or talk to your tax professional. In Chapter 21 I discuss ways to avoid or minimize the penalty.

If you overpay your estimated taxes, you are giving the IRS an interest-free loan. Not something you want to do when your business needs capital, the kids need shoes, or your beautiful trophy wife wants ass implants. It's also not something you want to do if you owe taxes for prior years to the IRS or the state, repayment to Social Security, back child support, parking tickets or other motor vehicle fees, or student loan interest. The IRS will not refund your overpayment; it will apply the money to those other obligations.

So before you buy that gorgeous Mercedes convertible, pay your estimated tax payments to the IRS and to the state (if you live in a state that levies income tax). You'll be glad you did. You'll have peace of mind, a good credit report, and the satisfaction of knowing that you are a good citizen.

Taxpertise Checklist

❑ Look at last year's income tax return to determine the liability you must prepay.

❑ Download Form 1040-ES and the corresponding state forms if applicable from irs.gov.

❑ If your income varies significantly from last year's income, then calculate and prepay the current-year liability.

❑ Check with your tax pro to pinpoint an accurate amount of estimated tax to prepay.

❑ If you are penalized for underpayment of estimated taxes, complete Form 2210 to reduce or eliminate the penalty.

5

Choice of Legal Entity

Decisions, Decisions, Decisions

*W*hen you start a business and at certain points during the life of the company, it's important to reflect upon the legal structure of the business. The basic legal forms to choose from include sole proprietorship, partnership, limited liability company (LLC), limited liability partnership (LLP), S corporation, or C corporation.

There are plenty of books with charts and graphs listing the pros and cons for each structure. The abundance of information is mind-boggling. And it's scary because making the right decision involves being a bit of a prophet. Much of the decision is based on where you see your company going. Will you have partners and what roles will they play within the organization?

The more formal the entity, the more time you and/or your partners will have to spend behind a desk playing by the rules. This is fine and dandy if you are cut out for this. But if you are always running short on office supplies, running short of patience, and running short of time to deal with paperwork, if you are a people person rather than a legal-pad-and-pen person, then having the wrong legal structure for your business could spell disaster.

> When making your decision about the legal structure of your business, push away those books with their charts and graphs for a moment and think about your emotional temperament and your relationship to money and paperwork.

Analyzing your temperament and inclinations to paperwork is definitely a starting point. Then take a look at those charts and graphs, preferably in the presence of your tax pro or attorney, to determine the legal and tax aspects of each entity and which would most properly suit your purposes.

Selecting an entity other than sole proprietorship will reduce your chances for audit. But please don't let that be your primary concern. There are far worse disasters than being audited. One of the greatest advantages of a sole proprietorship or partnership is the flexibility and simplicity of structure.

A corporate structure comes with a bucket load of paperwork and rules. If you are the type of person who is comfortable behind a desk, filling out forms and wielding a pen like a sword, or you can hire someone knowledgeable and trustworthy to do so, then you may be comfortable with this structure.

An LLC can be treated as a sole proprietorship, a corporation, or a partnership. If treated like a sole proprietorship, it will have the same audit risk but better asset protection in the event of a lawsuit (if you follow all of the rules).

Consider these psychological factors when choosing your legal form:

- Can I tolerate an abundance of paperwork and structure? (corporate)
- Do I tend to grab money from the business account when I need it? (sole proprietorship or partnership)
- Will there be outside investors and a plan to take the business public? (corporate, LLC)
- Is this a part-time venture with a potential for early demise? (sole proprietor, partnership, or LLC)

Before deciding, it's important to understand the tax structure and associated costs as well as the paperwork requirements of each entity. Oftentimes it is best to start simple as a sole proprietorship or partnership. Then later on when the business has proved successful, consider evolving into a more complex entity.

SOLE PROPRIETORSHIP

If you are just opening your business and you are the only owner, you may want to begin the enterprise as a sole proprietor. This is the simplest form of ownership with the least amount of paperwork. You cannot be an employee of the company, so there is no payroll unless you hire others. The basic requirement consists of keeping an adequate set of records in order to prepare a Schedule C, which will be attached to your individual income tax return.

Exiting from the venture is as simple as taking down your sign and walking away. No final returns to file, no documents to dissolve the entity. It's as easy as no longer filing Schedule C with your personal income tax return.

Sole proprietorship is generally the best selection while you are testing the waters and possibly suffering those inevitable losses associated with the first few years of operating a new enterprise. Those losses will offset other income on your individual income tax return.

How is a sole proprietorship taxed? Report sales, subtract business expenses, and pay tax on the difference, simple as that. The draws you took from the business are not part of the IRS equation.

Your bottom line (net profit) is subject to regular income tax. It is also subject to self-employment tax of 15.3 percent, which funds your Social Security and Medicare accounts.

Your chances of being audited are about 1.5 percent, which is higher than if the business were structured as its own entity, like a partnership or corporation.

PARTNERSHIP

Think sole proprietorship and add another person or two or more to the mix. You file a separate income tax return for the partnership. But the partnership doesn't pay tax. The profit is allocated according to your pro rata interest in the partnership on a form called a K-1. This form is filed with the partnership income tax return and a copy of it is sent to you with instructions about copying the numbers onto the various lines and schedules of your individual income tax return.

Your profit is subject to regular income tax and self-employment tax, same as a sole proprietorship.

CHOOSING THE ENTITY FOR YOU

Sole proprietorships and partnerships are fairly informal:

- Owners can grab money when needed (unless your partner slaps your hand).
- Owners don't have to be on payroll.
- If the business suffers losses, owners enjoy the losses on their own tax returns against other income (see your tax pro if you aren't actively working in the business; losses may be suspended).
- You don't have to hold board of directors meetings.
- A partnership files a separate tax return but taxes are paid at the individual level.
- Your chances of being audited are low (partnership only).
- Exiting from either entity is easy—take down the sign and walk away (partnerships must file a final tax return, which could involve taxable transactions).

Most of the problems associated with a partnership involve disputes among partners and other legal issues. So before jumping in, sit down with your attorney to hammer out an agreement with your partner(s). Most accountants will advise you not to go into partnership with anyone. It can be hell! If you are considering a partnership, make sure the other person is bringing something valuable to the party. Oftentimes a person creates a partnership with a person who has no money, no property, nothing to bring to the table. He may have expertise, but so what? Hire him as an employee. Why make him a partner if he has nothing concrete to offer but expertise? If you feel this person will bring more value than an average employee, then set up a bonus or commission schedule to reward the extra business or profit created by his efforts.

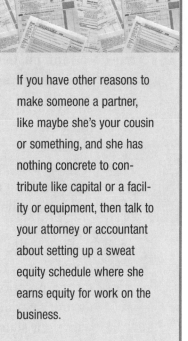

If you have other reasons to make someone a partner, like maybe she's your cousin or something, and she has nothing concrete to contribute like capital or a facility or equipment, then talk to your attorney or accountant about setting up a sweat equity schedule where she earns equity for work on the business.

C CORPORATION

Before incorporating your company, make sure you have a financially sound business that's going places. Your future should be so bright you have to wear shades. Incorporating is usually not worthwhile unless you are making a profit of more than $100,000 per year. If your only goal in incorporating is asset protection, think instead of increasing your insurance coverage.

Dan came to my office one day, big grin on his face. "I want to be a corporation." You'd think he was saying: "I want to nail that gorgeous chick."

I answered, "Whoa, hold up a minute. Becoming a corporation sounds very sexy. Automatic image and credibility. Asset protection. Yeah, it's all that, but it's definitely no bag of chips."

Dan wasn't good at paperwork. In fact, he barely got his tax return filed on time every year. He didn't want to deal with payroll, so he paid his secretary and other workers cash under the table. I don't know. Maybe Dan thought sporting *Inc.* after his company name would solve all of his problems. It didn't. In fact, Dan now has a stack of bills, notices, and letters from both the IRS and the state. He owes money, penalties, and interest. And the state has suspended his corporation.

For Dan, a corporate structure was an incompatible entity. Just like most beautiful mistresses, a corporation is high maintenance and can be very expensive. Here's how:

- As the owner-operator, you must be a corporate employee and must take your pay in the form of wages. That means obtaining federal and state ID numbers and hiring a payroll service.
- If you have a C corporation, you cannot write yourself a draw check without risking double taxation. That means the corporation doesn't get the write-off, but you've got to pay taxes on what you received.
- You must file a separate income tax return and pay a minimum franchise tax to the state as well as federal income taxes. Even if the corporation takes a loss for the year, the minimum state income tax must be paid. In California the amount is $800. Check with your state to find out how much it charges.
- You must hold board of directors meetings at least once a year.
- You must file other documents required by the secretary of state and pay filing fees on an annual basis.

If you become a corporation and do not follow these procedures, some really bad things may happen:

- The IRS could land on you and declare all those draw checks you took as dividends. It will change your individual tax return and hit you with a big tax bill including penalties and interest. An argument citing draws as shareholder loans will not carry weight unless accompanied by loan documents and a repayment plan that has been observed.
- Or, if you took draws and did not pay yourself proper wages, the IRS and the state may reclassify the amounts you drew as payroll.

They will hit you with payroll taxes, penalties, and interest and possibly a 100 percent trust fund payroll tax penalty.

■ If your corporation is sued and you haven't followed the rules, your personal assets may become targeted. Have you heard the expression "pierce the corporate veil"? That's just what opposing council will do. They will attempt to prove that you did not treat the corporation as a corporation. They will attempt to reclassify it as a sole proprietorship and expose your personal assets to the litigation.

Like I said, lots of paperwork!

If you incorporate the business as a C corporation and the business has losses, you cannot deduct the losses on your individual income tax return. You will have to carry forward those losses until the corporation makes a profit and then apply the losses to that profit.

By the same token, if you close down the corporation before it makes a profit, the losses die with the corporation and are not enjoyed against other income you make personally.

There must be a reason for people to incorporate. So what are the advantages?

■ Asset protection from creditors and litigants
■ Enjoyment of deductible fringe benefits like disability insurance, life insurance, and retirement plans within certain limits
■ Income splitting—creating a tax plan to juggle compensation between yourself and the corporation so that you enjoy the lowest corporate and individual rates

S CORPORATION

The S corporation enjoys a more flexible structure than the C corporation. As the owner-operator, you must be on payroll but you can also take advances against profits (dividends). Most of the fringe benefits available to C corporation employees are not available to owner-operators of an S corporation: for example, life insurance and disability insurance are not deductible. Retirement plan contributions and self-employed health insurance paid on behalf of owner-operators are deductible on your individual tax return even if the corporation pays those bills.

An S corporation does not pay federal income tax. It files a tax return but the profit or loss flows out on Schedule K-1 and is reported on your individual income tax return, much like with a partnership. But unlike a partnership or sole proprietorship, the profit is not subject to the 15.3 percent self-employment tax. That can be a huge tax savings.

However, keep in mind that because you are required to be on payroll, you will be paying into the Social Security fund. Anything above and beyond the amount you take on payroll is considered profit and will not be subject to the self-employment tax.

If you anticipate a profit of $100,000 for the year, don't think you can take only $10,000 in payroll and enjoy $90,000 in profit not subject to self-employment tax. Bear in mind that the IRS expects you to take "reasonable compensation."

Remember those attorneys structured as S corporations that the IRS audited just for this reason? There were quite a few who were taking payroll of $30,000, then raking in the remainder as huge dividends. The IRS did not consider the amount structured as wages as reasonable compensation. It hit the attorneys with a big tax bill after restructuring their compensation packages.

So check it out. Say you have $100,000 in profit and you take $50,000 as payroll. You have just saved about $7,500 in taxes (15.3 percent of the remaining $50,000 profit). That's a worthwhile trade-off for the extra paperwork and expense, isn't it?

In order to become an S corporation, it is imperative to file a Form 2553, Election by a Small Business Corporation, with the IRS no more than 2 months and 15 days after the beginning of your corporation's tax year. If you're a brand-new corporation, the beginning of the corporation's tax year is the date stamped on your certificate from the secretary of state. If your company is an existing C corporation, the date pivots around the beginning of the corporation's tax year, usually January 1. If this is the case, the due date is March 15.

If you incorporate your business using an online service or an attorney, follow up to make sure Form 2553 has been filed. You must sign the form and mail it in, so if it's not in the packet the incorporator gave you, give him a call. You might be told that your accountant needs to fill out the form. Hopefully, you have already discussed your intent to incorporate with your tax pro and she is on top of things—incorporating a business falls into the category of "Don't try this at home."

If you are late filing Form 2553, don't fret. You don't necessarily lose out on becoming an S corporation. You may file the form late with a letter stating "reasonable cause" for the late filing. Be sure to use that exact verbiage somewhere in the body of the letter. And your reasonable cause may simply be that you expected the person who incorporated your business to have performed this task. If you go to the IRS website, you will find instructions for completing this form and for remedying a late filing of the form. That's how often it happens! The IRS includes how to fix the situation right there on the instructions for completing the form.

Here's a sample letter:

Dear Sir:

Enclosed please find my signed Form 2553 for 123, Inc. Please note that the form is being filed late as the tax year began February 7, 20__.

The corporation has not yet filed a tax return. None of the shareholders are affected by the late filing of Form 2553, so there is no inconsistent treatment of any tax issue pertaining to the filing of this form.

I discovered this omission only recently. My attorney neglected to file this form and he did not advise me of the necessity of filing this form.

I therefore feel that this is reasonable cause for the late filing of Form 2553.

Please accept the late filing of Form 2553.

Thank you for your consideration in this matter.

If you make this discovery during preparation of the tax return, you may attach the Form 2553 to the tax return. There's a space on page 1 of the form where you can indicate your reasonable cause for the late filing.

Now that you've looked at the basic taxation elements and the psychological factors behind the selection of an entity, grab those graphs and charts and check out the other factors: fringe benefits, exit strategies, and asset protection, to name a few. Get out a legal pad and mark down the pros and cons as they relate to your business. Carefully analyze the factors and requirements behind each type of entity.

You may wish to offer the business plan on a cocktail napkin to your advisors prior to the meeting. This will give them a chance to think about your enterprise and form preliminary thoughts about the type of entity best suited to your business.

Here's an example:

Dear Tax Pro/Attorney:

I am starting a business called Topside Management, a temporary employment agency for paralegals. I will be the sole owner. Initially, I will be working from my home office. I have quite an extensive contact list and expect the business to grow rapidly. Within a year I expect to be located in an office downtown with a secretary and a staff of five. I see opportunities to franchise the business within five years. There are individuals in other states who are interested in opening similar operations. I plan to create a turnkey operation providing a standard operating manual, forms, and initial contacts to ensure their success. Within ten years, I will have sold off the whole thing and be living in Belize with my personal assistant, Javier, counting my millions. What legal form should my enterprise take?

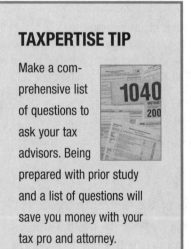

TAXPERTISE TIP

Make a comprehensive list of questions to ask your tax advisors. Being prepared with prior study and a list of questions will save you money with your tax pro and attorney.

With this information in hand, your attorney and tax pro can measure all the issues that pertain to the direction you are heading and help you decide on the proper course and advise you as to the legal entity that will cover your butt and minimize your tax liabilities.

If your attorney or accountant recommends incorporating, bear in mind that it would be a billing opportunity for him. Make sure he isn't suggesting an option out of a selfish interest. Ask your attorney why he thinks it's a good idea. If he responds, "Asset protection," ask if increasing insurance coverage would provide the solution. He may give you better answers revolving around issues like fringe benefit packages or exit strategies.

Also filter what an accountant has to say. He just might be thinking: "Money, money, money! If I incorporate this sole proprietorship, I'll get an extra tax return to prepare, a payroll client, additional tax planning sessions, secretary of state filings. Oh yeah! Let's do it!"

I'm not saying that every tax pro or attorney will pull that on you. The honorable ones will not. Most will analyze and judge your situation and try to give you their best advice. But it is my job to warn you about the sharp teeth out there. Educate yourself so you can participate more fully in making this decision. Do not blindly accept what any pro has to say. Question it, affirm it, and make it your own intelligent decision.

Be wary of those slick tax pros who advise you to incorporate in a state that does not levy state income taxes. If you do so, and your business is physically located in a state that does levy state income taxes, you will likely be required to file and pay state corporate income taxes in your resident state. Most states are very strict about this requirement. After all, you're doing business in your home state, your home state wants its share of those tax dollars.

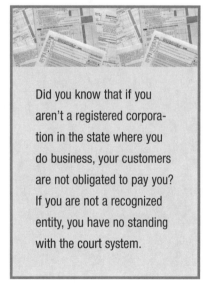

It doesn't matter if you set up a Post Office Box in Nevada or Delaware or in whichever tax-free state you incorporate; your home state will nab you if you so much as answer a phone there. It is not worth the penalties and interest or having to constantly look over your shoulder. And besides, some of the "tax-free" states, like Delaware, charge an annual fee for incorporating there. You might not save any money whatsoever.

Did you know that if you aren't a registered corporation in the state where you do business, your customers are not obligated to pay you? If you are not a recognized entity, you have no standing with the court system.

Taxpertise Checklist

❑ You already have a written business plan, right?

❑ Check your psychological makeup, ability to handle paperwork, and ability to follow rules against the requirements of each type of entity to determine which suits your temperament.

❑ Study the tax and benefit ramifications of each entity.

❑ Discuss your selection with your tax pro and attorney.

Hiring a Bookkeeper and a Tax Pro

Your Decision Should Not Be Based on Looks Alone

When I was 23 I applied for a bookkeeping position at a small construction company in San Francisco. The only experience I'd had in bookkeeping was keeping a DE ledger Grandma gave me when I was 10. I didn't learn until much later that DE stood for "double entry." I thought they were the initials of some famous accounting type, like the inventor of New Math.

I'd list my baby-sitting money in one column and how I spent it in the other. Not exactly dazzling resume material. Nor did it qualify me for an executive position with a top accounting firm. That was pretty much my accounting background. So with no experience, no clue, and a straight face, I applied for the bookkeeping job.

Hey, I look honest, was kind of cute, am real good at math, and am even better at talking smack, so I landed the job. On my first day, I pulled open the top desk drawer and found a stack of 20 or more employment applications from everyone I'd beaten out. And from the looks of the "Previous Job History" section, most of them had considerably more experience than me.

My on-the-job training consisted of me working alone in a cubicle trying to make sense of the numbers and wondering where to put them. There were plenty of old ledger books that gave me clues. I copied the format of what had been done previously. At the end of each quarter, Ernie, the CPA, would drop by to pick up the ledgers. He was a timid, mild-mannered little man with big, funny glasses. I would barrage him with my list of accounting questions. I rather think he enjoyed these mentoring sessions. I know I did; I learned more from him than I ever did in college. And maybe he had hopes for me, because I don't think he ever tipped off my boss about my lack of skills.

Pretty soon I wasn't faking it anymore. I knew what I was doing. Within a year, I was nearly qualified for the job. Funny how my boss, an extremely intelligent and successful man, had no clue otherwise.

You know what? He's no different than most employers who know their product or service but don't exactly know if their bookkeeper is doing the job accurately and correctly. Not to mention honestly. An employer may hire an applicant who has prior job experience or comes highly recommended. Doesn't mean a thing. The applicant still may not be qualified. Unless the employer has an accounting education or experience, he will likely not know for sure if the person he hires is really qualified to do the job.

I've seen the following expensive judgment errors occur over the years:

■ A bookkeeper claims she has payroll experience but really has none. She shorts the payroll tax deposit every month because she is not aware that employer taxes must be paid with the paycheck withholdings. Big tax bill, penalties, and interest.

- A bookkeeper throws away the sales tax form instead of filling it out because he's not sure what it is. More penalties and interest.
- A bookkeeper misclassifies many transactions, neglects many others, and doesn't reconcile the bank account. The person preparing the tax return has to do the books over again so they make sense. Wasted money.
- A bookkeeper uses Excel spreadsheets to create busywork. QuickBooks remains unused; the bank accounts aren't reconciled. The boss knows his checking account balance only because he checks it online every day.

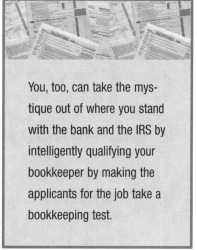

You, too, can take the mystique out of where you stand with the bank and the IRS by intelligently qualifying your bookkeeper by making the applicants for the job take a bookkeeping test.

The best way to ensure competency is to require that each applicant take a bookkeeping test. Figure 5.1 is a test complete with answer key. Feel free to give this test to anyone applying for a bookkeeping job with your company.

The test will measure the basic skills of a candidate for the position. The true-or-false section tests for basic knowledge. The calculations section tests for logical thought process and algebraic skills. The third section tests the applicant's knowledge of debits and credits and his ability to classify transactions. If an applicant can complete the exam in 45 minutes and answer most of the questions correctly, then chances are that you have found a qualified bookkeeper.

The honesty part? Don't have a test for that one. You'll have to do your own profiling, fingerprinting, and research.

Decide if you need a bookkeeper full time or part time. List the tasks you want the bookkeeper to accomplish and determine how much time each one takes. This may include bill paying, bank reconciliation, and payroll processing.

Figure 5.1 *Bookkeeping Test*

BOOKKEEPING SKILLS EVALUATION

Name: _____

True/False Section

1. _____ An owner's personal expenses paid from a sole proprietorship business account are posted to draws, an equity account.

2. _____ Parking fines incurred in the course of doing business are deductible business expenses.

3. _____ Wages earned in December 2009, but not paid until January 2010, must be accrued and included on the employee's W-2 for 2009.

4. _____ Capital and net worth are increased when the business shows a profit.

5. _____ A 1099-Misc form must be sent to independent contractors if payments to them for services exceed $300 for the year.

6. _____ When posting a partial payment on a credit card, it is best to allocate a percentage of the payment to each expense account reflected in total purchases made on the credit card statement.

7. _____ When expenses are not paid for at the time they are incurred, they are recorded as liabilities.

8. _____ Payroll stubs are not required to be given to employees so long as the proper taxes are withheld, the earnings are reported to the taxing authorities, and the records are made available to the employee(s) for review.

9. _____ Monies owed to creditors of the business are known as accounts receivable.

10. _____ Withheld FICA taxes from an employee's pay must be matched by the employer when making federal tax deposits.

11. _____ Loan proceeds deposited to the business checking account are taxable income to the business.

12. _____ The balance sheet is a financial statement that reflects the sales for the period.

13. _____ Equipment possessed by a business is called an asset.

14. _____ Accounts receivable is known as a current asset.

15. _____ Utilities costs are a common deductible business expense.

Figure 5.1 *Bookkeeping Test,* continued

BOOKKEEPING SKILLS EVALUATION

Calculations

1. _____ Gross sales (sales + sales tax) are $3,195. The sales tax rate is 6.5 percent. What is the amount of sales tax included in the gross sales figure?

2. _____ If interest at 6 percent for a full year on a principal sum amounts to $12, what is the principal sum?

3. _____ The bank statement received for a business account as of the end of June shows a balance of $3,414.92. Items not reflected on the statement are check #2516 for $57.28, check #2517 for $83.99, as well as a deposit from June 30 for $516.00. It is discovered that the bank cleared a check written during June for $157.95, not $175.95 as recorded in the checkbook register. The bank statement lists monthly service charges as $15.00. What is the reconciled balance of this account?

4. _____ It's payday. John worked 40 hours. His rate of pay is $12 per hour. The FICA rate is 7.65 percent. Other taxes to deduct amount to $160. A $100 repayment of an advance on pay will be deducted. What is John's net pay?

BOOKKEEPING SKILLS EVALUATION

Matching

Read these instructions carefully. Below is a list of accounts in the general ledger. Using the letter in front of each account title, make journal entries for the transactions listed below for this *accrual basis business.* Indicate the letter (or letters) of the accounts to be debited first, then

---

Figure 5.1 *Bookkeeping Test,* continued

---

indicate the letter (or letters) of the accounts to be credited, separating all debits and credits with a hyphen. **Example: GP-A**

A Cash	**J** Sales
B Accounts Receivable	**K** Sales Returns
C Equipment	**L** Bad Debt Expense
D Accumulated Depreciation	**M** Depreciation Expense
E Deposits	**N** Discounts Expense
F Accounts Payable	**O** Interest Expense
G Sales Tax Payable	**P** Office Expense
H Notes Payable	**Q** Telephone Expense
I Capital	

1. _____ A wholesale customer returns merchandise purchased on account for credit.

2. _____ A retail customer pays $53.25 cash, including sales tax, for merchandise.

3. _____ We are posting $150 for equipment depreciation this month.

4. _____ One of our customers declared bankruptcy and the customer's debt of $500 to us was canceled.

5. _____ We pay our 30-day note to the bank for $500 plus $60 interest.

6. _____ We pay $98.14 for a COD delivery of office supplies.

7. _____ A customer pays $24.50 on an invoice for $25, taking advantage of our 2 percent, net 10 terms.

8. _____ We have purchased a copy machine, paying $500 down and financing the remainder of $1,745.

9. _____ We received the telephone bill on December 19, but will not be paying it until the due date of January 15.

10. _____ The telephone company returned our $100 deposit paid five years ago when the business began operation. The funds were deposited into the checking account.

11. _____ A sole proprietor won the lottery and deposited $20,000 into the business checking account.

Figure 5.1 *Bookkeeping Test,* continued

ANSWER KEY

True/False

1. True	6. True	11. False
2. False	7. True	12. False
3. False	8. False	13. True
4. True	9. False	14. True
5. False	10. True	15. True

Calculations

1. $195.00

2. $200.00

3. $3,789.65

4. $183.28

Matching

1. K – B	5. HO – A	9. Q – F
2. A – JG	6. P – A	10. A – E
3. M – D	7. AN – B	11. A – I
4. L – B	8. C – AH	

Interview questions for a prospective bookkeeper include the following:

1. Have you ever used (your brand name) accounting software?
2. Have you ever been arrested and convicted of a crime, like embezzlement?
3. What were your duties at your last job?
4. Do you have experience with processing payroll? (if applicable)
5. Have you ever prepared a sales tax return? (if applicable)
6. Do you have experience with ____ (List any other required duties you expect the bookkeeper to perform.)

TAXPERTISE TIP

If you decide to hire a bookkeeping service to come in monthly, set up  a box labeled "Bookkeeper." Throughout the month, toss in all items you want the bookkeeper to deal with— bank and credit card statements, loan documents, insurance renewals, workers' compensation questionnaires, bank deposit receipts, receipts for major asset purchases, notes, requests, and questions.

Oftentimes it may prove less costly to hire a bookkeeping service. Your chances of obtaining a highly skilled and efficient individual are enhanced. You may be pleasantly surprised to find that even if the hourly rate is substantially higher, the cost may be less. This is because the individual is more highly qualified and experienced and therefore is more efficient and works faster.

Most bookkeeping services will accommodate you with monthly on-site visits. The bookkeeper uses your computer and software—no back-and-forth with discs and e-mailed files. Every file she needs is handy, which reduces processing time and therefore your cost.

A tax pro is the next person to hire if you are self-employed. It's great to have a basic knowledge, but tax law is complex to the point of being burdensome.

Not only can a tax pro prepare your income tax return, he can give you tax advice and create tax plans to project and minimize your liabilities.

Licensed tax pros fall into three main categories:

1. *State Licensed Tax Preparer*. This person took the eight-week H&R Block class or something similar. This is junior level. If you have a W-2, you're fine. If it gets more complicated than that, you might be dealing with someone who knows enough to be dangerous. Believe me, I speak from experience. We all start somewhere.

> Hire a tax professional. You have better things to do than memorize and interpret all 14,000-plus pages of the tax code.

2. *Certified Public Accountant*. A CPA is licensed by the state and probably has a college degree in accounting. Some CPAs consider tax return preparation a sideline. Perhaps she specializes in 1031 exchanges or internal audits. If she prepares taxes as a business mainstay, find out if she has a particular area of expertise. Perhaps she specializes in real estate or small business or trusts and estates. Be sure her area of expertise aligns with the basic content of your tax return.

TAXPERTISE TIP

The IRS is more likely to audit a self-prepared tax return than one prepared by a professional. It makes sense. The IRS expects that a tax pro will exercise due diligence and apply income tax law correctly.

In fact, as I look back over a 25-year career of defending folks in audit, I'd have to say that the number of tax returns I prepared that were drawn in the audit lottery number was about three. Most of the audit representation work came in as referrals from existing clients or other tax practitioners.

3. *Enrolled Agent.* Enrolled Agents focus on taxation issues and are licensed nationwide to represent taxpayers at all levels within the Internal Revenue Service. They, too, may specialize in certain areas of taxation, so be sure to inquire.

When looking for a tax pro, ask a friend or relative with a similar financial situation for a referral. Then call the tax pro. A preliminary discussion will reveal if she is the one for you.

Interview questions for a tax professional:

1. *Are you aggressive or timid in your interpretation of the tax law?* Throw something out to get an idea of where this tax professional stands, such as, "Do you believe my home office is a red flag?" (Answer: Not any more, if you follow the rules.)

2. *If I am audited, will you represent me?* A lot of tax pros merely want to prepare tax returns; their fears of dealing with the IRS are equivalent to yours. Or they just may hate the hassle. Most tax pros have another gig along with preparing taxes. Some of them opt for financial planning, others write mortgages (well, maybe before 2008), and some write books (Ta da!) and do representation work.

3. *If I get into tax trouble, will you intervene with the IRS on my behalf?* See number 2 above.

4. *Are you a CPA, EA, or licensed tax professional?* Please make sure you are dealing with a licensed individual. Tax law is very tricky, and self-proclaimed experts who are not backed up by credentials can put you in some scary situations.

5. *Do you do handle many tax returns for my industry and legal form?* This is an age of specialty. I have an attorney who specializes in real estate, but when it came to doing a real estate 1031 exchange, he wouldn't handle it. Ask how much experience the tax professional has in dealing with clients in your particular situation, for example, "I'm self-employed working from a home office. Do you handle many self-employed individuals?" Test the person's knowledge. Ask if there any tax law changes that pertain to your situation.

6. *Is your office open year round?* You might have a quick question, need some tax planning, or require help with correspondence from the IRS or the state about your tax return. You definitely want to make sure the sign is still standing and someone answers the phone on November 12 when you receive an audit notice!

7. *Will you charge extra if I call with a "quick question"?* I love this one. The phone rings and one of my clients is on the other end. "I've just got a quick question," she says and then proceeds to ask the tax ramifications of exiting from a ten-year series of 1031 exchanges. Yeah, it's just as hard as it sounds and it involves lots of math and spreadsheets. Well, guess what? That's not a quick question. That's a project. And someone's getting billed for it. But if a client calls and asks, "What's the mileage rate this year?" OK, now we're talking about a nonbillable quick question.

A competent bookkeeper and tax pro on your team will give you peace of mind and save you money. The fees are not inexpensive, but believe me, the amount of money they may save you in penalties and interest to the IRS and other taxing agencies may make it a break-even proposition.

Taxpertise Checklist

❏ Determine if you need a bookkeeping service, a part-time bookkeeper, or a full-time bookkeeper.

❏ Interview and test all applicants.

❏ Interview tax pros and find one who is knowledgable about your situation.

Cozy Business

7

My Hobby, My Business

Or I Always Wanted a Pony

*D*ebbie is a full-time nurse who has a passion for Andalusian horses. She found a piece of land, built a barn and corrals, added half a dozen horses, and opened a horse breeding operation. The startup and operating costs were killers and she sustained huge losses year after year. But Debbie is an optimist. She just knew that someday, maybe in a galaxy far away, she would succeed. She would rake in the big bucks and make a name for herself among the horsey set.

She didn't quit her day job; she couldn't afford to. She happily suffered losses and long hours devoted to this occupation. After all, she loved her horses and she loved the work.

Debbie filled out Schedule C and wrote off the losses from the breeding business against her big fat W-2 salary, substantially reducing her tax liability. In fact, she was getting some pretty sweet refunds, which, of course, she dumped right back into the breeding operation.

The IRS is suspicious of losses for enterprises that are inherently fun: horses, yachts, airplanes, limos, quilting, photography, golf— anything that smacks of a good time. Its initial reaction is "This isn't a business; it's a hobby!"

> The bad news is that you can't take a loss on your tax return if your "work" is classified as a hobby.

If the work you're doing is classified as a hobby, you can deduct your losses only up to income received. In other words, the best you can do with a hobby is break even. No tax savings there! So if the IRS can reclassify your loss as a hobby loss, your tax bill will climb.

Most people are under the impression that you must show a profit in the past three out of five years or five out of seven years for horse breeding, training, showing, or racing for the enterprise to be deductible. They believe the rule is carved in stone and is automatic. That's simply not true.

The activity will be questioned if it does not make a profit during at least three of the last five years, including the current year. An exception is training, racing, breeding, or showing horses. Such activities are considered a business if it's profitable during at least two of the last seven years.

The operative word here is *questioned*. Big difference, right? The loss is not automatically disallowed. You are given a chance to prove that the enterprise is a business, not merely a hobby that pulls in a few bucks from time to time.

Well, the IRS figured Debbie was having way too much fun with her horse breeding activity, so it sent the auditor from hell to put a stop to it.

The auditor voiced the following arguments:

- There is no serious profit motive.
- Debbie works full time in an unrelated profession.
- There's no mileage log to support the vehicle expense deduction.

If it smells like a hobby, it is a hobby, the auditor concluded.

I fired back with a QuickBooks general ledger and financial statements to prove Debbie maintained business records. I showed the auditor an appointment book with destinations from which we could compile a mileage log. Then I pushed a file of advertising clippings to sell the foals that were born over the years, a business license, and business loan documents across the desk. The entire package spelled *profit motive*.

> The IRS has its own opinion about tax write-offs that sound like fun. "Horses, humph! She probably always wanted a pony and now she thinks she can write it off? I don't think so!"

Finally, I elaborated on Debbie's struggle. Debbie had not had a decent vacation or even a weekend off in years. All of her time and effort were devoted to the horses. Instead of spending weekends and holidays partying, she was mucking the stalls. Instead of buying Manolo Blahniks for herself, she was paying a blacksmith for new shoes for Thunder and Gypsy.

And Debbie's hard work was finally beginning to pay off. Business was looking up. In fact, on her most recent tax return, the loss was substantially lower than in prior years. And if we eliminated the deduction for depreciation, which is an accounting adjustment rather than an out-of-pocket expense (writing off a portion of the cost of the stables and the cost of the horses she paid for in year one), there would have been a profit.

The auditor exhaled loudly. " Fine! I'll allow the losses."

If the losses had been disallowed, Debbie would have owed almost $100,000 in back taxes, penalties, and interest for tax returns filed the previous three years in which she had declared losses. This can be some serious stuff!

Say you're an amateur photographer with a great eye for composition, color, and form. A friend offers you a couple hundred bucks to photograph her wedding. You're not doing anything else on Saturday, so off you go. You do a great job and enjoy yourself as well. The bride is blissfully pleased with the results and spreads the word about your talent. Now her aunt wants you to photograph her son's birthday party. Wow. This could be a good thing—money in your pocket and free cake!

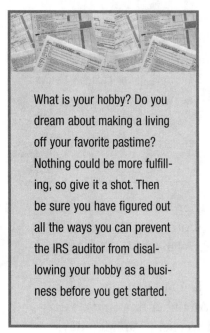

What is your hobby? Do you dream about making a living off your favorite pastime? Nothing could be more fulfilling, so give it a shot. Then be sure you have figured out all the ways you can prevent the IRS auditor from disallowing your hobby as a business before you get started.

You start thinking: "Why not turn this into a part-time business venture?" You might not want to quit your day job. Not yet anyway. But this new career track might have potential. Wouldn't it be thrilling to have a studio with your name on it someday or a lucrative side profession to pursue in your dotage? So you print some business cards and start networking.

The thing is, these first couple of years, you'll likely not turn a profit. I mean, you made a little cash on the wedding and the birthday party. But overall, your expenses exceeded your income. The camera alone cost $900, the memory card another $50, then there's gas to get to and from both events. Not to mention the dry-cleaning bill to get all the red wine out of that white shirt. And those business cards set you back about 50 bucks. You're getting a couple hundred bucks for a photography gig, so it's not like you can quit your day job.

And so you wonder, "Can I declare this income and write off all these expenses against it?" If your intent is to treat this as a business, the answer is yes. Simply attach a Schedule C to your tax return listing your income and expenses. The loss you generate will result in a reduction to your tax liability.

If you are devoted, it doesn't matter if the business is only a part-time venture; the losses will be allowed. However, it is important to prove that this is a business, not just a hobby from which you sometimes make a few bucks.

The three-out-of-five-years rule (or two-out-of-seven) applies to individuals, partnerships, trusts, estates, and S corporations. It does not apply to corporations other than S corporations.

Incorporating a business primarily to avoid a hobby loss audit is not a good idea.

If you go to the trouble to incorporate as a C corporation, your losses will not come under scrutiny with regard to the hobby loss rules. This doesn't mean the IRS won't want to look at your tax return for other reasons, however.

Other factors to consider if you incorporate as a C corporation are the additional paperwork requirements, the minimum franchise tax charged by your state government, and the fact that the losses can't be taken on your individual income tax return. It could, however, be one very small factor to consider when you make your selection of a legal entity.

If the IRS disallows your losses, the tax benefits you enjoyed will disappear. Not only that, but the IRS will backtrack three years and disallow prior losses, which can result in a very expensive tax bill.

Your hobby income will be allowed, of course. The IRS is more than happy to tax it. Your deductions against that income can be listed on Schedule A under miscellaneous itemized deductions. If you don't have enough to itemize deductions, and instead take the standard deduction, you will lose these additional deductions.

If you want to keep deductible losses on your tax return, you need to fill out Schedule C. In order to do so, you must be running a bona fide business and be ready to prove it in case you are audited. Here are a few pointers:

- *Prove a serious intent to operate as a business.* Give the business a name to identify it as a business entity. For example, Incredible Images Photography Studio.
- *Obtain all required licenses and insurance.*

■ *Demonstrate a businesslike attitude.* Open a separate checking account under the business name. Deposit all business income and pay for all business expenses from this account. With the exception of subsidizing the business account with personal funds, do not co-mingle personal and business transactions.

■ *Operate like a business by maintaining a set of books and records.* For approximately $100 you can purchase accounting software or even use an Excel spreadsheet to properly record transactions and evaluate profits and losses.

■ *Demonstrate a profit motive.* Advertise your product or service. Keep a file folder marked "Advertising" to store clippings of all ads you have placed. During an audit this will go a long way to show that you are a serious player.

■ *Improve your skills.* Attend conventions and trade shows; take classes and workshops. Keep all fliers and registration forms in case of an audit.

■ *Network.* Join the chamber of commerce and other professional organizations. Pay the dues from your business checking account.

■ *Keep a journal of your sales activity, contacts, connections, and efforts made to promote your business.*

■ *Maintain a mileage log.* This will not only substantiate your vehicle deduction, but it will demonstrate a desire to play by the rules.

■ *Chart future projections and plans to turn the activity into a profitable enterprise.* Evaluate why you are experiencing losses. Then change the way you carry on your business in an effort to become profitable. One of the key factors in determining whether the activity should be classified as a hobby or a business is your dependency on the income it generates. If there is no profit stream, the IRS will conclude that you must enjoy it so much it doesn't matter if it's profitable. Hence, it's a hobby. You must prove that you are working hard to develop your enterprise into a business.

■ *You want to show the reason why this enterprise should be considered a business.* Perhaps we're talking about a career change. This will replace your day job or will become a source of income in your retirement years. Like the horse breeding enterprise, it may just take lots of money and time to develop into a profitable business.

An auditor once asked, "If this is a serious business, why isn't he making any money at it?"

I shrugged and answered, "He's a lousy businessman." Because I provided proof of intent to make a profit and books and records to show the enterprise had been handled like a business, the auditor simply nodded and allowed the losses.

If you follow the previous guidelines, you will likely be successful in proving to the IRS that you mean business!

If you are starting a business that you expect will be scrutinized by the IRS in a hobby loss audit, you can keep IRS agents off your back until year five (or seven) by filing Form 5213, Election to Postpone Determination as to Whether the Assumption Applies That an Activity Is Engaged in for Profit. Now isn't that a mouthful! This is a simple one-page form that asks for a brief description of the activity, your name, address, legal form, and the year the activity began. The key is to be brief. There is no need to be defensive, offer apologies or excuses, or add any other wording that makes it appear you are guilty of any wrongdoing. If you are opening a photography studio, then simply write in "Photography."

The benefit of filing this election is that the IRS will not immediately swoop down to perform a hobby loss audit. It will wait until the five (or seven) years is up before taking a look-see. This gives you a chance to turn a profit or abandon the venture before the time limit elapses. Even if you abandon the business, you may be audited. But as long as you have conducted the enterprise in a businesslike manner, you have nothing to fear.

Taxpertise Checklist

❏ Examine how you conduct your business to ensure that it will not be classified as a hobby.

❏ Follow the guidelines in this chapter to audit-proof the business in order to deduct losses on your tax return.

❏ File Form 5213 to prevent audit during the inception and first five years of the enterprise.

8

Home Sweet Home Office

Where Every Day Is Casual Friday

I don't think there is anything more fun than working out of your house. Most of the time you can sit around in your pajamas until 10 o'clock in the morning and crank out a project—kind of like what I did as I wrote this.

If the phone rings, you can answer it oh so professionally and the unsuspecting party on the other end has no clue that you have rocky road ice cream all over your face and a washing machine churning away in the next room. You can sing out "Vandaley Enterprises" a la George of *Seinfeld* fame, and the caller will assume you're in a crisp, tailored suit with a red power tie on the 14th floor of some Manhattan skyscraper.

In fact, I got my first client while wrapped in a bath towel with my hair dripping from the shower. "So, uh, and what are you wearing?"

If you have decided to work out of the house, you can enjoy these benefits:

- *The convenience*. At 2 A.M. when you can't sleep, you can finish up that nagging proposal. Or at noon when you've had it, you can take a break, make a bowl of popcorn, and flip on a *Sex in the City* rerun. While your long, long document is printing out, you can start a load of laundry.
- *Cost savings*. No extra rent and utility bills to pay, no signage cost, no commuting costs like gas, tolls, or parking.
- *Time savings*. Your commute may involve only dog and cat traffic in the hallway.
- *A really nice tax write-off*. Allocating home office expenses to the business, even if you can already write off mortgage interest and property tax, will save you money in self-employment taxes.
- *You can write off other expenses that normally are not allowed*, like homeowner's or renter's insurance, utilities, repairs, and part of the housekeeper's pay, to name a few.

In the recent past, people viewed those who had home offices with disdain. Anyone working out of her house wasn't taken seriously, was not considered very professional. And in fact, even the IRS was suspect of those who attempted to deduct their home offices. They pictured some guy using his dining room table to write a few reports or do a little bill paying, clear it off in time for the family meal, then try to write off half his housing costs. The IRS spent a great deal of time slapping these folks around and letting them know that they would not be allowed to take advantage. But the times they have a-changed.

There are two tests that one must pass in order to deduct a home office: exclusive use and principal place of business.

In 1990 a self-employed anesthesiologist named Nader Soliman tried to write off his home office. He had no office space at any of the three hospitals where he provided services. He needed a place to bill his clients and perform other administrative chores, do research, read medical journals, schedule and console patients, and consult with other physicians. He furnished one bedroom of his three-bedroom apartment with a complete office setup. He didn't use this room for any other purpose and therefore met the first test: exclusive use.

The IRS disallowed the deduction stating that he failed the second test. His home office was not his principal place of business. Well, duh, I don't think the good doctor is going to arrange to have his patients be put under anesthesia in the home office. How are you going to get to the hospital after Dr. Soliman puts you under? By the same token, the only place Dr. Soliman will provide his service is in the operating room. So even if he rented an office downtown or in one of the hospitals, which would be deductible all day long, he would not put patients under in either of those office settings either. The IRS auditor gave him a dense stare and told him he couldn't take the deduction.

Dr. Soliman fought tooth and nail all the way to the Supreme Court and, amazingly enough, he lost.

This decision was a major headline for tax practitioners and all self-employed people nationwide. This meant that anyone who didn't practice his career from his home office could not take the deduction. Suddenly contractors, landscapers, real estate agents, outside sales reps, and anesthesiologists, among others, were losing a valuable income tax deduction.

The impact was huge; almost everyone with a home office went into shock. Seemed like only computer nerds and bean counters could take the deduction simply because we spend most of our day in the home office. (Oh, hey, lucky me!)

Consider this: If you can't deduct your home office because you don't spend the day there, you can go up the street and rent an office space and deduct it even if you're an electrical contractor who is on the road all day and only makes a pit stop to check mail and pick up messages. What the hell is that? Totally unfair, that's what.

After the Soliman decision, tax pros lived in fear. You know how people love to shoot the messenger.

We were allowed to exhale in 1999 when the IRS came to its senses. The home office was back.

But there was a new development. People were scared. Terrified. They feared taking the deduction. "Red flag, red flag! Don't do it!" they cried. And here we are a decade later and many taxpayers still cannot be cajoled into taking the deduction.

Here's the deal: The red flag is pretty much gone with the exception of blatant, cheating abuse. Now, more than at any other time in history, people are working from their homes. Not just self-employed individuals but wage earners, telecommuters, independent contractors, and freelancers as well. In a report to Congress, the Taxpayer Advocate Office stated that use of a home office jumped 20 percent between 1999 and 2005.

The IRS knows and accepts that the home office is commonplace these days. It also knows that the Soliman decision was unfair and has repented its unreasonable stance. It took down and folded up the red flag and tossed in into the garbage where it belongs.

If you have a bona fide home office, take the deduction! Take every deduction to which you are entitled. The only worry is if you don't follow the rules or if you attempt to fudge a bigger deduction than what you are entitled.

There are two main requirements to determine if your home office is deductible:

1. The area must be used exclusively as a home office. Personal use is not allowed. If you admit to using your home office computer to download porn, you will blow your home office deduction out of the water. If the room you are using is multi-purpose (like a den that doubles as a television room or an office that doubles as a guest room) you may deduct only the area that is devoted exclusively to home office activities.

2. The area must be used on a regular basis and be the principal place of business for your company. The interpretation of this rule is now different than when the IRS nailed Soliman. Basically, you cannot have an office or store or plant elsewhere and have a home office as well. The room you are deducting must be the main place

where you do your work, meet clients, and so on. If you have an office or store downtown and bring work home, you do not have a qualified home office and should not attempt to take the deduction because it won't qualify as your principal place of business. If you work for The Man, and he provides office space for you but you bring work home, even if it's every night, you do not have a valid home office deduction. The office is deductible only if your boss requires that you have the office space and does not otherwise provide you with office space. Get a letter from your employer stating that this is the case and keep it in your tax file in case you are audited.

So how do you determine the deduction? First of all, you have to figure out the ratio of home office to the remainder of the house. Divide the square footage of the office space by the total square feet of your home.

If your home is 1,200 square feet and your office space is 120 square feet, your ratio is 10 percent (120 ÷ 1,200 = .10). Apply the 10 percent ratio to the following costs:

TAXPERTISE TIP

Include areas where you store tools and inventory but only the amount of space that's used exclusively for that purpose. If you use part of your garage, then include the square footage of the storage area, not the square footage of the entire garage.

- Mortgage interest or rent
- Property taxes
- Homeowner's or renter's insurance
- Utilities—gas and electric, garbage, water, propane
- Cleaning repairs and maintenance (this could be 100 percent deductible if the cost is specific to the home office)
- Telephone—if the only phone line is the home phone, the IRS will accept the home office percentage applied to the total of the home phone bill
- Depreciation of home office and all major capital improvements that affect the home office, for example, new roof or hot water

heater multiplied by the home office percentage. (But if, for example, you install new carpet in the home office only, the entire cost will be used as the basis for depreciation.) Report these figures on IRS Form 8829.

If you own your home, it would be wise to defer depreciation calculations to a tax pro, at least for the first year. Calculating depreciation can be a tricky business. The tax pro can provide a depreciation schedule outlining what your deduction will be every year.

TAXPERTISE TIP

Take a depreciation deduction for the furniture and equipment you use in your home office. Maybe you have a desk and a chair, bookcases, filing cabinets, and shelving units that were previously for personal use. Now they are business assets and can be written off. Use the lower of cost or fair market value as the basis for depreciation. Here again, I would suggest deferring these calculations to your tax pro. Keep pictures in your tax file in the event you are audited.

Write off expenses that are shared between family and business. If clients come to your home office, you likely have a bathroom for their convenience. You may deduct a pro rata share of the supplies and cleaning products dedicated to that room. But do not include the bathroom in your square footage calculations if it is shared with other members of the family.

CHILD-CARE PROVIDERS

Child-care providers use a different standard when determining how much of their home can be deducted for business use. It's called the time-space method. Because the kids run rampant throughout the house, it's possible you have a 100 percent business use of the entire house, but not 24/7. The business use is limited to the hours the business serves the children.

In that case, determine the total square footage of the home, then deduct any areas that are off limits to the kids. Also, deduct and figure separately any areas that are 100 percent exclusively used for business. This could be a playroom that only the day-care children use (don't try it if you have kids of your own), a home office (subject to the home office rules) where you do the books, plan the meals, and research the internet for activities, a storage area where you keep sleeping mats, toys, and other items used only in day-care activities. Put the exclusive use number aside for the time being.

The nonexclusive areas like the hallways, kitchen, living room—all areas used by your family as well as by your tiny clients—will be subject to a calculation based on the hours used for business purposes.

Look at Form 8829, which can be found at irs.gov. There are 8,740 hours in the year. Do the math to determine your time-space percentage of the nonexclusive areas. You will add to that the 100 percent business use of the exclusive areas to come up with the total percentage to apply to your expenses.

Make sure you track the business use time for a minimum of two months for substantiation purposes in the event of an IRS or state tax audit.

The formulas for business use are complicated if you run a day-care center out of your home. I can only hope that your head didn't spin off and hit the wall. If you prefer, visit a tax pro with your raw data and let her determine the formulas and percentages relating to your exclusive and non-exclusive business use for day care.

TAXPERTISE TIP

Don't forget to include the time you spend as a day-care provider talking to parents in person or on the phone, bookkeeping time, putting away groceries and preparing meals, planning meals and activities, internet research, cleaning, and so on. Any time you spend on the business itself translates to an increased business usage percent and tax-dollar savings.

TAXPERTISE TIP

A child-care provider can also depreciate a portion of all major assets: living room furniture, refrigerator, stove, electronics (DVD, VCR, stereo equipment) used in the shared space. If you do not have purchase receipts for the assets, you may determine a fair market value—basically a garage sale value—for the items in question. Then list them, total them, and take photos in case you need to substantiate your deduction in an audit. Apply the time-space percentage to these items to determine the basis for depreciation. Any of the items used 100 percent for business, such as a play structure (if you have no kids of your own), should be separated and indicated as such so that you use 100 percent of the cost for depreciation. You would not apply the time-space percentage to items used 100 percent in business.

Taxpertise Checklist

❏ Be sure your home office is used on a regular basis and exclusively as your principal place of business.

❏ Figure out the percentage of business use by dividing office square footage by total square footage of the entire house (e.g., 120 ÷ 1,200 = .10 or 10 percent).

❏ Depreciate or expense everything in your office.

❏ Don't forget to write off pro rata expenses shared with family expenses.

Business Deductions

What Is Business Income?

And, Do I Have to Pay Tax on That?

*M*ark brought his shoebox full of receipts and bank statements so I could
compile his income and expenses and do his taxes.

"Do you have any sales invoices? Sales records?" I asked.

"Nah, just take the total of the bank deposits," he said.

I compiled the data and began preparation of the tax return. When I compared the results with those of the prior year, I was surprised. His sales had
almost doubled, which seems strange in a service business unless you hire

employees. He hadn't. And there are only so many hours in a day. So I perused the bank deposits and found one for $20,000 and another for $30,000. Didn't look like sales. The rest of the deposits were pretty much under $5,000, and they weren't nice round numbers like these two.

I called Mark. "Oh yeah," he said. "My sister lent me 20 grand. And the other one, let me think for a second here. Yeah. I borrowed money from the credit union to buy another truck."

"Well, Mark, those loans aren't taxable income. They don't belong on the tax return."

"They're not? But I used the money for the business."

"Doesn't matter, Mark. They're loans, not sales. Dang, did you know that if I let that tax return fly out the door, you would have paid an extra 10 grand in taxes that you didn't have to?"

Mark was shocked. Then grateful.

TAXABLE BUSINESS INCOME

Let's check in for a moment about that very first line on your Schedule C, partnership income tax return, or corporate income tax return: sales. Several times each year I see a potential overpayment of taxes because business owners do not understand that the only business income subject to tax is derived from sales and a few other transactions explained later.

Loans, credit card cash advances, funds transfers from personal accounts, and overdraft protection from a credit line are not taxable income. How do those tax-free transactions end up on the tax return? Because, like Mark, a taxpayer will tell his tax pro, "Add up the bank deposits on my business checking account statements. Those are my sales for the year." There may be nontaxable income mixed in with the bank deposits. It happens more often than you think. It is important to separately track sales from other sources of income so you don't pay extra tax. Aren't you hit hard enough already?

Funds from otherwise taxable sources (interest, dividends) should not be included with sales as business income and therefore taxed on Schedule C if you're a sole proprietor. List this income on Schedule B of Form 1040.

You may ask, "What's the difference? It all shows up as income on the tax return anyway." True; however, all of the income listed on Schedule C is subject to 15.3 percent self-employment tax as well as income tax. Dividends and interest are subject to income tax only. It doesn't matter if the account is in the name of the business. Interest and dividend income is not subject to the self-employment tax.

If you include interest and dividend income on Schedule C, the IRS will let it ride. It will not send you a correction notice and a tax refund. It is up to you to know the tax law and apply it properly. Besides, how does the IRS know your sales figure includes the bank interest you earned?

By the same token, if you do not separate dividends and interest to Schedule B, you may receive a letter from the IRS asking why you didn't report the interest or dividend income. A bill for the additional tax will accompany the letter. It's so much easier to do it right from the get-go.

Income to list on line 1 of your Schedule C, partnership, or corporate income tax return includes the following:

- *Sales.*
- *Rents.* Rents from personal property if that is the principal business activity of your company
- *Royalty income.* If you hold an operating oil, gas, or mineral interest or are self-employed as a writer, an inventor, or an artist, you report your royalty income and write off your expenses on Schedule C. I say this to differentiate from the line item for royalty income on Schedule E. Royalty income on Schedule E is strictly from copyrights and patents for which you have no discernible expenses.
- *Bartering.* Bartering is taxable! In fact, you must send out a 1099-Misc by January 31 to report the value of any trade for the prior year. Include the value received as sales.

Under "Other Income" on line 3 of Schedule C, include the following:

- *Sublet income.* If you sublease any of your shop or office space to others include the sublet income. You'd probably love to show it somewhere else on the tax return to avoid paying self-employment tax on it, but that wouldn't be appropriate. The reasoning is that you have expenses to match this income, namely rent and utilities that you pay for the entire space. So the income belongs with those expenses on Schedule C.

- *Finance charge income.* This includes such income collected on delinquent accounts receivable customers.
- *Discounts.* Discounts include early pay discounts you enjoy from vendors, if you show the full amounts under the expense category.
- *Refunds.* List refunds from insurance companies and others, if the deductions were taken as business expenses.

Sale of business assets like trucks, furniture, and equipment is generally listed on Form 4797 and Schedule D. This income is subject to capital gains taxes, which are usually a lower tax rate than income taxes. These transactions are not subject to self-employment tax. However, a part of the sale attributed to depreciation recapture may be subject to income taxes. The equation can be a bit tricky, so you might want to check with your tax pro.

If you trade in a business property, say a truck or equipment for a new truck or a new piece of equipment, you may be able to escape paying taxes on the trade-in because of the like-kind exchange rules. Again, talk to your tax pro.

Rebate income from business purchases is not taxable income, but you must reduce the basis of any business property by the rebate amount. If you bought a truck for $25,000 to use in the business and you received a $1,000 rebate, then the depreciable basis is $24,000. Don't include rebate income on Schedule C.

OTHER TAXABLE AND NONTAXABLE INCOME

Now that we've covered what income must be included on Schedule C, let's look at the taxability of other income streams. The following incomes are not taxable.

Inheritance

If Granny Bee leaves you a million bucks in cash, God bless you (and her!) and keep on rolling. It seems to surprise a great many people to discover that an inheritance is usually not taxable. The IRS takes its share, believe me. Normally, the tax is levied at the estate level, not the beneficiary's level. In some cases, if the estate isn't required to pay the tax, the beneficiaries may have to. If so, you will receive a Form K-1 from the estate or the trust indicating your share of the income on which to pay the taxes. Perhaps there aren't enough assets to require an estate income tax return. Let's say that's the case with Granny Bee. Granny Bee passes but doesn't have a million bucks. She leaves you her little house. She paid $25,000 for it back in the day. That number will not be part of the equation. An appraiser comes out and says the house is now worth $200,000. You decide you want the cash instead of the house, so you sell it for $200,000. Those are the two numbers in your equation. Your profit is zero. You have no tax liability in this case. If you sold the house for $225,000, you would pay taxes on the $25,000 profit.

One exception to the rule is if Granny Bee leaves you the money in her IRA account. This money has never been taxed. The IRS wants a piece of it when it changes hands. But it has laid down some rules to make it easy on the beneficiary and to increase the time period over which the taxes must be paid. If you are the lucky recipient of an inheritance, I would suggest that you visit a tax pro to discuss the ramifications.

Any money earned off inherited property is taxable. If Granny Bee leaves you a savings account and you let it ride, you must pay taxes on the interest it accumulates.

TAXPERTISE TIP

If you want to leave part of your estate to charity, then donate the funds in the balance of your retirement account. A bona fide charity does not pay taxes and, unlike other beneficiaries, will not have to pay taxes on the retirement account.

When it comes to estate tax law, there are no simple answers, only complex situations. So check it out with your tax advisor.

Life Insurance Proceeds

These are not taxable unless the policy was turned over to you for a price.

Public Assistance Programs and Disability Benefits

Benefits received from welfare, public assistance, or disability programs are usually not taxable. A part of them, usually compensation for services in a work program, may be taxable. Or disability benefits may be taxable if someone other than you paid the premiums.

Child Support

This is not taxable income. Nor is it a tax deduction if you pay it.

Physical or Emotional Distress Compensation

Physical injury or sickness compensation and emotional distress settlement awards stemming from a lawsuit are not subject to income tax. If the emotional distress is personal and stems from, say, an unlawful discrimination, breach of contract, or other such mental wronging, then it is taxable income.

Scholarships and Fellowships

These are not taxable if they are for tuition, fees, books, supplies, and equipment required for courses at an educational institution. Amounts attributable to room and board are taxable.

Taxable—Maybe, Maybe Not

The following income is taxable or it falls into the category of "it depends:"

■ *Cancellation of debt.* Having debt cancelled is an indirect way of getting money for free and therefore is taxable income unless you are bankrupt or can prove insolvency. You will receive a Form 1099 from the creditor showing how much debt was cancelled.

- *Foreclosure debt.* Because of the massive number of foreclosures in recent years, the tax laws have changed. There is a formula that may help eliminate or reduce the amount of taxable income from debt forgiveness.

- *Student loan debt.* If you had a student loan with a provision to cancel the debt if you work for so many years in a particular field, the loan forgiveness is not taxable.

■ *Recoveries and reimbursements.* These items are taxable if they were ever once a deduction. For example, if you write off a customer's bill to bad debt and take the deduction on your tax return and the customer shows up a year or so later and makes good on the debt, you must show that amount as income. Or if you receive a refund from the state on filing your tax return, the amount might be taxable if you took the payment of state taxes as an itemized deduction.

■ *Unemployment compensation benefits.* Yes, these will kick you while you're down. When you file for unemployment, you have the option to have federal withholding deducted from your benefit check. Most people can't afford to do so. But the following year, especially if you received benefits for a long period of time, you might be looking at a big tax bill.

■ *Hobby income.* You must declare hobby income as taxable income. You can take deductions against it only if you itemize deductions. The deduction amount cannot exceed the total income you declare.

■ *Alimony.* Although child support is not taxable, alimony is. A new concept termed *family support* makes the topic a bit more complex. Check with your tax pro about your particular situation.

■ *Punitive damages.* These are taxable income even if the settlement arises from a physical injury or sickness.

■ *Gambling winnings, lotteries, and raffles.* You'd better believe this is considered taxable income. You'll likely get a 1099. It's a good idea to track your losses because those are deductible to the extent of your winnings. You can't deduct more losses than winnings, how-ever. Many casinos provide a method of tracking your losses, so take advantage of that just in case you hit the jackpot. If you win a noncash prize, like a trip or a car, you must include the value of the prize in income and pay taxes on it.

- *Kickbacks.* A kickback is are basically a commission on a sale and must be included in taxable income.
- *Rewards.* These are taxable.
- *Profits on personal property.* If you sell any of your personal belong-ings for a profit, you have to pay capital gains taxes on it. Operative word here is *profit*. Usually, that doesn't happen. You buy a refrigerator for $500. Twenty years later when you're sick and tired of it and harvest gold is no longer in, you sell it for $50. You don't have to report the $50 because it isn't a profit. If you sold the refrigerator to some rube for $600, then you would have to report the transaction on Schedule D and pay taxes on the $100 profit.
- *Illegal profits.* Any bribes or ill-gotten gains from criminal activities are considered taxable income. If you steal property, you must pay taxes on the value of the stolen property. This is how the IRS nailed Al Capone. In 1913 the tax law read that one must pay taxes on all "lawful" income. Shortly thereafter, "lawful" was struck off the code because too many crooks were laughing in the face of the IRS. Can you picture it? I robbed a bank! Sure ain't lawful income! Tax free! Yahoo!
- *Distributions from retirement plans.* These monies are taxable and may be subject to penalties if taken before age 59½ unless an exception applies. A part of the amount received that represents after-tax contributions is not taxable.
- *Honors and awards.* And finally, when you win the Pulitzer or Nobel Prize, you've got to pay taxes on it!

This is not the full extent of the tax law concerning taxable versus nontaxable income. The examples I show in this chapter represent the most common types of income that are received. If you receive other forms of income and wonder if they are subject to income tax, contact a tax pro or visit the IRS website at irs.gov.

Taxpertise Checklist

❑ Learn what income is taxable and what income is tax-free.

❑ Be sure to issue 1099s to clients with whom you barter.

❑ Keep sales records; don't rely on the total of bank deposits.

❑ Track interest and dividends separately from sales.

Just What Can I Deduct?

Can I Call My Dog a Business Expense?

*T*alk about opening up a subjective area for debate. The IRS allows you to deduct "ordinary and necessary" expenses. Boy do I love to debate what falls under that category. There is nothing more satisfying than turning an auditor's doubts into full understanding of why a dubious-sounding expense is really ordinary and necessary. Apply logic and plenty of documentation, and voilà! You may have a deductible business expense. Hey, you may even think your dog is an ordinary and necessary business expense.

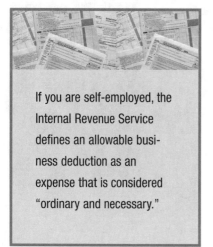

If you are self-employed, the Internal Revenue Service defines an allowable business deduction as an expense that is considered "ordinary and necessary."

The following are examples of expenses that might be business deductions for one but considered nondeductible personal expenses for another. What it boils down to is whether it is ordinary and necessary as it applies to your specific business operation. A second element to consider is *intent*.

Sherry, the Hairdresser

Sherry is a hairdresser whose Schedule C business is audited one year. The auditor has no problem allowing the deduction for a subscription to *Vogue* magazine. The cost of the subscription is definitely a job-related, research expense as well as an acceptable client expense. You can walk into any hairdresser's salon in America and find a copy of *Vogue* or some similar beauty magazine. Clients should be entertained while they are waiting for their appointment or sitting under the heat lamps. And a client may find a hairstyle on page 87 that she wants to try. That makes the magazine subscription an ordinary expense.

It's good business to provide this form of entertainment to a client. Imagine how many clients would switch hairdressers if there were no magazines to peruse, no cup of coffee to sip. That makes the expense necessary. Sherry's deduction flies without a raised eyebrow from the auditor.

Sandy, the Caregiver

Sandy is self-employed as a caregiver with only one client. When she attempts to write off the subscription to *Vogue* because she reads it while her client is asleep, the same IRS auditor says, "Hell no!" Reading *Vogue* is a time filler not related to the job itself. The content of *Vogue* is not job-related; therefore, the intent is personal.

Secondly, the subscription is not an ordinary expense. A blood pressure cuff would be an ordinary expense for a caregiver, but *Vogue* magazine? Not. It doesn't matter what kind of spin Sandy wants to put on it.

"But I read it at my job." That doesn't make it job-related. "Sometimes I read it to my client." Hmmm. Getting warmer. Might even fly.

Still, the auditor may respond, "So? Reading *Vogue* magazine is not a job requirement nor does it contain specific information to maintain or improve your job skills." The auditor is also thinking, "I bet Sandy gets paid while she's sitting there on her big butt reading that trash. Hell, I can't read *Vogue* on my job. If she thinks she's going to get a deduction for that, she's got something else coming!"

An exception based on intent would be if Sandy bought the subscription as a gift for her client. Then it could be classified as an allowable job-related expense. Business owners are allowed to purchase gifts of up to $25 per client or employee per year. Purchasing gifts for clients is an ordinary and necessary business expense in that it creates goodwill and promotes satisfactory working conditions.

If Sandy had purchased a subscription to *Caregiver Today* to read while her client slept, that would be considered job-related and therefore deductible.

Lisa, the Web Designer

Lisa designs websites and successfully writes off her *Vogue* magazine subscription because her clients, beauty supply stores and beauty salons, enjoy a *Vogue*-style format and require up-to-date beauty data for their web pages. The subscription is a valid research expense, job-related, and therefore deductible. Of course, the auditor can only suspect that Lisa's gorgeous hairstyle was one she found on page 87, cut out, and ran with to Sherry, her hairdresser. Lisa won't open her big mouth and admit there was any personal enjoyment whatsoever.

You see what's going on here? A *Vogue* magazine subscription may or may not be a write-off. It depends on the facts and circumstances that support whatever deduction you are taking. Is the intent business or personal? Is it ordinary and necessary in your particular industry?

Here's an even better example and a true story: A topless dancer attempted to write off the cost of her breast implants as a business deduction. The IRS said hell no! So she took the case to tax court and won!

The judge at tax court undoubtedly realized that no strip club owner was going to hire a flat-chested dancer. A general contractor wouldn't hire a carpenter that didn't have a tool belt and some tools to shove in it. Got to have the tools of the trade. The dancer has to have something to shake, right?

Let's assume this same woman were an outside sales rep rather than a topless dancer who insisted that she needed the implants to look good for her job and to help secure more sales. The auditor, the tax court magistrate, and the Supreme Court justice would roll their eyes and say, "Hell no! It's not a valid business expense." Then they would tell her that psychiatric fees to restore her self-esteem would be deductible.

Does it work as a medical expense? Hell no again, because cosmetic surgery is not considered a valid medical expense. Even there, the IRS looks at intent and necessity. If a woman went through a mastectomy and required reconstructive surgery to restore her once beautiful breasts, the expense would be a deductible medical expense. Correction of physical disfigurations is deductible because of the potential psychological damage living in such a physical state could cause.

Do you see what's happening here? Every deduction that comes under scrutiny may be allowed or disallowed depending upon the intent of the taxpayer and the necessity of the deduction as it pertains to the class of deduction—whether for business, for medical purpose, and so on.

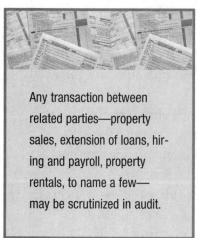

Any transaction between related parties—property sales, extension of loans, hiring and payroll, property rentals, to name a few—may be scrutinized in audit.

There is no definitive list of authorized business deductions in the IRS code, regulations, or procedures. There are a few ifs, ands, and buts sprinkled throughout the code—a few guidelines mostly on the "No" side of the column. The term "generally" is also used quite a bit.

We've looked at "ordinary and necessary" business expenses. We've also looked at business intent versus personal intent. The IRS also looks at deductible expenses in terms of whether they are "reasonable." This concept arises usually when one is dealing with related parties. Related parties extend beyond family members. If you are a shareholder in a closely held corporation, you and the corporation are considered related parties.

The auditor is looking for fair compensation, judged by factors such as fair market value and willing buyer, willing seller. A deductible transaction between related parties may be disallowed if the compensation is not reasonable.

For example, a shareholder borrows money from his corporation. If the corporation does not charge interest or demand a repayment plan, the IRS will reclassify the loan as a dividend and therefore taxable. The shareholder, who enjoyed the loan as tax-free income, will now have to pay taxes on it. The corporation does not get a deduction because the payment of dividends is not deductible. This is the origin of the term *double taxation*.

Wages paid to a related party will be scrutinized to determine if the amount paid is reasonable. Rents paid, 1031 exchanges, and sale of assets, among other transactions, are examined if conducted between related parties.

"Lavish and extravagant" is another phrase the IRS uses mostly to determine the deductibility of entertainment and meals expenses. Even there, special circumstances and factors prevail. What is considered lavish and extravagant to someone making $30,000 per year may be completely different than it is to one who takes home a million bucks a year. The IRS can't tell you how to live. If you want to fly first-class on a business trip and you have the means to do so, then do it and write it off.

So let's take a look at what you cannot deduct on Schedule C (sole proprietor), Form 1065 (partnership), or Form 1120S (S corporation). Most of these rules apply to C corporation entities. However, some rules may be different, especially when it comes to fringe benefits. Check with your tax advisor for specifics.

■ It almost goes without saying, but I will include it here. Any personal expenses with no business purpose are not deductible. However, the business portion of expenses that are part business, part personal can be apportioned and deducted. For example, if you pay interest on a loan or credit card where the funds are mixed use (business and personal), apply the business percentage to the annual interest and take the amount as a business deduction.

■ If you provide health insurance for your employees, you may deduct this cost under fringe benefits. But the amount you pay for yourself, partners, or S corporation shareholders or employees is not deductible as a business expense. You do not lose the deduction. It goes on the front page of the individuals' Form 1040 under adjustments to income. In fact, check to make sure you or your tax pro has been taking this deduction on your behalf. After all, this is on the list of often-overlooked deductions. Deduct the premium only to the extent of profit. If your business is showing a loss, the entire deduction will be included under medical expenses on Schedule A.

■ Life and disability insurance are not deductible anywhere on your tax return (exceptions apply for C corporations) even if they're required by your partners, shareholders, or lender of business debt. Life insurance premiums paid for employees are deductible as long as you or anyone who has a financial interest in the company is not the beneficiary.

■ Cash donations belong on Schedule A—Itemized Deductions (there's an exception for C corporations). It doesn't matter if you write the check out of the business account; it's considered a personal deduction.

If you are getting something back for the payment, such as advertising in the school yearbook for funding the softball team, then it is not a donation. It is an advertising expense and is deductible on Schedule C.

If you write a check from the company account to a charity and receive a gift for making the donation, you must subtract the value of the gift from the total donation, unless the gift itself can be considered a business expense; in that case, allocate that portion to your Schedule C. A straight-up, here-you-go, no-strings-attached donation is not a business deduction (exception for C corporations). For a partnership or S corporation the donation amount will be included on the business tax return but the amount will flow through on your K-1 and will end up on your Schedule A—Itemized Deductions.

- Donations of your time have no value to the IRS even if you are donating business services for which you would ordinarily charge. No deduction, not on Schedule A, not on Schedule C. However, if you donate inventory from your business, you may deduct the fair market value (not your cost!) of the donation on your business schedule. When those silent-auction fundraisers come around, donate inventory. Your business enjoys some well-deserved free advertising and you get more bang for your buck on your income tax return.

- Monies paid for illegal activities are not deductible. Kickbacks, bribes, parking tickets, speeding tickets (I had to speed to get to the client meeting on time, then I parked in a red zone) are not deductible. I heard of a case where a business owner paid an arsonist to burn down his store for the insurance money and deducted the payment to the arsonist under outside services. I wonder if he sent the arsonist a 1099 for services rendered. When the business owner was audited by the IRS, it all came to light and he not only was disallowed the deduction but served time for the crime.

- Clothing, makeup, haircuts, manicures, pedicures, and facials are not considered ordinary and necessary business expenses no matter how important you claim your appearance is. I don't know how many carpenters have tried to write off their blue jeans—can't do it. They can write off their T-shirts as an advertising expense if the company name is emblazoned thereon. Many outside salespeople want to write off their business suits. "I have to look good for the job," they cry. Clothing is deductible only if it is a uniform, protective gear, or a costume required by the job and not suitable for everyday wear. If you're in show business, that's a different story. Check with your tax advisor to see what you can write off. A member of Rod Stewart's band was disallowed a deduction for his stage clothing because it was considered suitable for daily wear. It was all glitter and color and crazy style. But then he was a freak, so the IRS figured he looked like that all the time.

If you work outdoors you may write off the cost of sunblock, sunglasses, and hats. Those items are considered protective gear. Apportion the expense between business and personal use, however.

■ Gifts are deductible up to $25 per year, per employee or client. This rule has been around forever with no adjustment for inflation. Please note that there is a big difference between gifts and entertainment. If you want to reward someone for a value higher than $25, think in terms of a nice dinner out or an entertainment event rather than a gift.

■ Your dearly beloved pug, Sweetie Pie, the one with the bad eyes who just celebrated her 14th birthday, is not considered a valid security expense. It amazes me how creative folks can be. Cindy owns a little boutique in a wealthy area of town. Every day she carts in her little pug dressed to the nines in the latest doggie fashion. Hell, this pug is more doll than dog, more froufrou feminine than Reese Witherspoon in *Legally Blonde*. She's also a very old blonde and ready for assisted-living facilities. Her deaf little ears don't register the chimes when shoppers enter. Half the time you wouldn't even know that Sweetie Pie is in the shop. Unless she's asleep. The drunken-sailor snoring emanating from the lacy pink bed below the cash register gives her away. "So can I write off Sweetie-Pie's clothes and vet bills?" Cindy asks.

"As what? Your dependent? I don't think so," I respond.

"Well, no, duh, she's an animal. I mean as security expense for the shop?" Cindy says with a straight face. Unbelievable. Doesn't crack a smirk. I raise my eyebrows and look at her over my readers. She shifts a bit in her chair, but still no smirk. "I'm serious," she says. "Tandy next door writes off her ferret."

I snort. "I can't do that. Remember, I've met this dog. If she even spotted someone entering the shop, she'd likely lick them to death.

And that ferret? She writes off that ferret? All that ferret ever did was poop on the merchandise."

▪ Hiring your kids can be a good way to save tax dollars via income splitting. If the child is under the age of 18, his wages are not subject to FICA, Medicare, FUTA, or SUTA. However, be sure that the kids are there working and making the money. It is not a write-off to simply allocate an amount at year-end. As with any other expense, have proof of payment and time sheets to prove that they actually put in the hours.

DEPRECIATION AND AMORTIZATION

Depreciating is writing off an expense over a period of more than one year. If you buy a box of paper clips, you would write off the full amount on your tax return the year in which you bought the box of paper clips. However, if your business purchases a capital asset—that is, something that adds significant value to the business: equipment, vehicles, furniture, and fixtures—the useful life is more than one year.

The IRS requires that you write off the capital asset over its useful life. IRS Publications 534 and 936 contain tables of useful lives and acceptable depreciation methods. Essentially, equipment and vehicles are written off over five years, furniture and fixtures over seven years, your home office over 31.5 years.

Prior to 1987, depreciation was a fairly simple matter. You essentially divided the cost by the useful life. The result would be the depreciation deduction for each year. There were a few other methods available but those were fairly simplistic as well.

Today's methods are a bit more complex and change often, so I suggest you check with your tax pro. IRS Publication 936, which deals with depreciation methods, is 112 pages long! How crazy is that?

A special note about vehicle depreciation: If the vehicle is not considered "transportation equipment" like a dump truck or boom truck or a hearse—that is, if it's a vehicle that can be used personally as well as for business—you are limited in the amount of depreciation that you can take over the vehicle's useful life of five years. For example, if you purchase a vehicle that costs more than the "luxury car limit" (this amount changes annually but it's only about $15,000) prescribed by the IRS, the depreciation period will be longer than five years.

The IRS got tired of seeing $100,000 Ferraris listed as business vehicles with the accompanying huge write-offs. Plus back then, you could write off a vehicle over three years rather than five. They changed the law, adding in the luxury car limits and making the rules and depreciation calculations a tricky business.

There is, however, a special accelerated depreciation method called Section 179 in which you are able to write off substantially more the first year. This applies only to purchases of new assets and only to assets purchased during that particular tax year. You cannot apply Section 179 to assets purchased in prior years.

If you take the Section 179 deduction or elect any depreciation method other than straight line for the first year for a vehicle, you cannot ever use the standard mileage method for taking vehicle expenses in any future year.

Congress changes the Section 179 limits from year to year, so check with your tax advisor to find out what the current amount is. In 2008, Congress passed an incentive for business in which it raised the limit from the 2007 level of $125,000 to $250,000 or $285,000 if your business is located in an Enterprise Zone. Sometimes first-year bonus depreciation is available. Check with your tax pro or the IRS website for up-to-date information, methods, and rates.

Claim depreciation, bonus depreciation, and Section 179 deductions on Form 4562. The total from the form is then moved to your Schedule C and deducted from your business income.

If you sell a business asset, consider the tax hit. You must recapture the depreciation you deducted and pay regular income tax on it (not the preferred capital gain rate). The reason you pay regular income tax rather than capital gains is because when you took the depreciation deduction, you enjoyed a reduction of tax based on the regular income tax rates.

Amortization is similar to depreciation but it's applied against intangible assets—stuff you can't physically see, like goodwill, client lists, and points. The write-off period is generally longer than it is for assets like equipment, furniture, and vehicles. For example, goodwill and client lists are written off over a 15-year period and points are written off over the life of the loan. If you paid points for a 30-year mortgage, you must write off those points over 30 years.

The Section 179 deduction is not available for amortization.

Because the rules and methods are complex, I would advise you to consult with a tax pro about depreciation and amortization rules and calculations, especially if you intend to prepare your own tax returns. Let a tax pro review your assets and prepare the schedules to ensure compliance.

The last and most important thing to understand about business tax deductions is *take them*! "I paid cash but I can't find the receipts," and "I'm not sure what that ATM charge is on my bank statement; I guess you should just show it as draw," and "Business insurance? Oh wait, I forgot about that. I think I charged that on my Visa card but didn't book it" are phrases I often hear from clients. There are possibly hundreds and thousands of dollars not deducted every year because the receipts don't hit the books.

TAXPERTISE TIP

If you purchase a business, the purchase price must be allocated among the assets you receive. You need this breakdown in order to prepare your income tax return. The business you purchased is a combination of various assets, all of which are deductible through depreciation or amortization over their useful lives. You enjoy a larger write-off each year if most assets are classified as equipment (5 years), then furniture and fixtures (7 years), then covenant not to compete and goodwill (15 years). The Section 179 election is not available for any components of the purchase of a new business.

Or they don't hit the books because there are no receipts. A good example of this is car washes. I go to a local car wash where I pay cash and never get a receipt. It's a couple of guys with towels and brushes and a drive-through machine. These guys don't have any paper on them. I'd never even dream of asking them for a receipt. They'd probably shoo me off to the 76 station if I did.

Because I use my car 80 percent for business, I can deduct $8 of the $10 I pay for the car wash and tip. That's $8 a week in deductions, about $400 a year, which translates to a tax savings of close to $200. So what do I do? I mark "CW $10" in red in my appointment book. I add it up every month and show it as an expense on my financial statements and on my tax return. What if I'm audited and have no receipt? I can show the auditor my appointment book and if necessary, argue about it. "I mean come on, see this French manicure? Do you really think I wash my own car? I'm such a prima donna—you've got to know I'm not driving around in a mud-packed Beemer, right?" He will likely allow the non-receipted deduction. And if he doesn't? Oh well. I gave it my best shot but got shot down. I can always appeal the decision to the auditor's manager.

Replace bad habits with simple systems so you get every deduction to which you are entitled. Think about those business meals where the cash receipt disappeared, those car washes, those cash fill-ups at the gas station, the quick stop at the drugstore to buy a box of staples. It can add up to a substantial amount in the way of tax savings. And adequately document any business expense that smacks of personal use in order to win at audit.

I don't know about you, but I'm going out right now to buy a pair of really cute shoes with that $200 I just saved on my car wash deduction!

Taxpertise Checklist

❑ Think about questionable deductions in terms of ordinary, necessary, intent, not lavish or extravagant, and reasonableness.

❑ Talk to a tax pro about depreciation, amortization, and Section 179 expenses.

❑ At the end of each month, book all expenses paid in cash, personal credit cards, and checks to your business accounting program.

Vehicle Expense

Don't Attach a Clipboard to Your Steering Wheel

*D*an, a new client, arrived at my office for his tax appointment. He had dutifully filled out the tax organizer I had mailed to him. His penmanship was like a draftsman's—perfectly aligned, square, and consistent.

I flipped to the first page of data. Dan had copied every figure from every box of his W-2 onto the organizer despite my telling him he needn't do that. Just give me the W-2; no need to do any copy work. And, like most tax pros, I prefer to work from the document itself. The numbers written onto an organizer could possibly be transposed or illegible. Hey, no problem. Lots of folks like to mark up the organizer; I just hate to see them go to all that extra work.

I flipped a few more pages and found that Dan has a side business as a computer consultant. He has a home office and travels quite a bit to his clients' places of business. I turned to the home office worksheet, and lo and behold, Dan had actually prorated his mortgage interest, insurance, property taxes, and utilities between personal and business use of the home. Poor guy. Another waste of time since the tax software does that for me automatically.

When I turned to the section regarding business use of the automobile, my eyes bugged out. You'd think I'd found a black widow squashed onto the page. What I saw was something I had never seen before and have not seen since: A complete six-page mileage log detailing to the tenth of a mile every destination by date for the entire year. Beside it was listed Dan's actual expenses, including gas, vehicle registration, repairs, insurance, and auto loan interest. He listed his grand total mileage, his commuting mileage, his personal mileage, and his business mileage. Absolutely amazing.

It is rare for a client to list his automobile expenses because most clients don't track their costs during the year. Rare for a client to even know his total mileage. But to show every expense plus attach a mileage log with so much detail wasn't just rare—it was a once-in-a-lifetime event. With any other client, even the most anal retentive of the lot, the page is usually blank. And it's typically accompanied by this conversation:

Me: So, Bob, did you use the van this past year in your mobile repair business?

Bob: Yep.

Me: So how many miles did you drive, Bob?

Bob [His head rears back and his eyes dart skyward as though the answer were inscribed on the ceiling. In fact, I think it would be great fun to take a marker and write "19,497" right up there above the client chairs.]: Uh, I don't know. Probably about the same as I did the year before. How many miles did I drive then? Whatever it was, add another thousand.

As if mileage inflation ran side by side with economic inflation.

Dan was the client from heaven by comparison. All I could do was stare at the mileage log. Dan shifted in his seat and cleared his throat.

I finally picked up my jaw from the desktop and closed my mouth. Where did I put that box of gold stars? I wanted to offer Dan a job. What else do you do with someone like that? I mean, there would be no lost files, ever. Every client conversation would be documented in great detail. Every figure on a tax return would be backed up by tapes and logic and citations of tax code and photographs and schematics. He would be the perfect employee. I wouldn't have to spend years carrying on about the importance of documentation. He already got it.

It was either that or ask him what the hell is wrong with him. Find out if he was being treated for obsessive-compulsive disorder and, if so, did he remember to include a deduction for his meds?

I didn't do either. I simply prepared Dan's taxes and have enjoyed a smooth and steady business relationship with him ever since.

Naturally, Dan never got audited. So I never had the pleasure of making an IRS agent's eyes bug out the way mine did.

The funny thing is that what Dan brought me is exactly what the IRS wants. Or so then say. IRS regulations dictate that if you are using a vehicle for business purposes, you must keep a contemporaneous mileage log, which means you're supposed to mark down your mileage as it occurs. That's what Dan did. Dan and Dan alone in the entire country, in the entire universe, if in fact they have taxes on other planets.

The IRS can require us to keep logs all it wants. Just like our parents required us to make our beds and be home by ten and not hit our siblings. But let's get real. Dan is the only guy out there who does this. The rest of us don't have the time or inclination for this busywork. Like we're really going to stare at our odometers and mark down ".8" every time we have to run over to the office supply store. As small-business owners, we're spending our time changing hats and putting out fires. No time for crayons and clipboards. Sorry.

For that reason I will not lecture you about keeping a log. I know you won't do it. Even if you make it a New Year's resolution and you're gung ho, I'd bet you dollars to martinis that by January 15, you'll be off the wagon.

It's damn near impossible to keep up that good habit. Well, guess what? IRS agents are reasonable human beings and most of them agree with me—no one's going to keep a damn log. Every IRS agent I've dealt with over the past 25 years, even the most hard-boiled of the lot, the ones who have the look of disdain down pat, the perfected eye roll, the smug eyebrow raise, even they have agreed to allow reconstructed logs.

Unless you're Dan, here's what you should do: First off, even a reconstructed log needs a starting point. It's very simple. Write your beginning odometer reading in your appointment book on January 1, and in bright red, mark "odometer:" on the December 31 page so you remember to record the ending reading at year-end. Now subtract one number from the other to find out your total mileage. It looks so much more believable and accurate to see 14,823 on the tax return under total mileage than it does to see 15,000, which is a dead giveaway that the student hasn't done her homework.

Try as much as possible to note all business meetings, errands, and other business vehicle travel in your appointment book. In fact, if you can do it, track both business and personal miles for a two-week period every quarter. Keep the info in your tax file for use at year-end to determine the ratio of business versus personal use.

Provide the total mileage figure and business mileage to your tax pro.

Some people think they can get away with writing off 100 percent of their only vehicle for

TAXPERTISE TIP

If you use an electronic device or computer to track your schedule, enter the information the same way you would list an appointment. If possible, at the end of the year print out your electronic schedule to store in your tax file in case of audit. Maybe you can impress the auditor the way Dan would have had he been audited.

business. All they are doing is tempting fate. Bob is one of those. Remember him from a couple of pages ago? He's such a bad boy; he keeps no records. Here's the rest of our conversation:

Me: OK, Bob. So how much of the mileage would you say is personal?

Bob: Oh, I don't have any personal mileage at all.

Me: But Bob, you don't have another vehicle.

Bob: Oh I know. But all my miles are all business.

Me [Heavy sigh. We go through this every year.]: But Bob, you certainly must go to the grocery store or have a girlfriend somewhere.

Bob: I do grocery shopping on the way home. And my girlfriend Susie? She does all the estimates and paperwork.

Me [eye roll]: Right. What about weekends? Don't you have 49ers season tickets?

Bob: Yep, but that's a business expense, too.

Me: OK, Bob, whatever. Fine.

Bob thinks I'm going to give him 100 percent. But he's wrong. I know that old van is not 100 percent business use. So I knock off some points when he isn't looking and figure we're pretty square with the IRS.

So what is business mileage? First of all, you cannot deduct commuting. So forget about driving from home to your primary business location or from home to your first client. An exception is if you are self-employed and have a qualified home office. Your commute would be defined as travel down the hall or through the yard to the space that serves as your office. Once you are in the office, then every destination to which you travel to carry on business is considered business mileage.

See the logic? After all, if you have a regular job, you never deduct your commuting mileage against your W-2 wages. Once you get to work, if your boss requires that you use your vehicle for business travel, mileage for which you are not reimbursed is deductible.

You may also deduct travel between jobs. If you have two employers, you can deduct the mileage for travel from job No. 1 to job No. 2.

Just don't stop at home first. That will blow the deduction out of the water.

I often walk from my home office to the post office and sometimes to nearby client offices. On one such walk, I wondered how audacious it would be to write off my shoes. Maybe I'd have to keep pedometer readings in my appointment book to substantiate business use. Hey, why not? I bet, however, that my Manolo Blahniks wouldn't be considered an ordinary and necessary business expense. The IRS would likely reduce that write-off to what one would spend for a pair of hiking boots, if they allowed the deduction at all. I can hear the auditor now: "You of all people should know better."

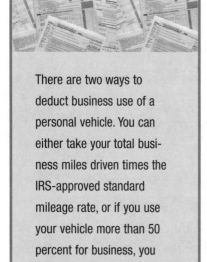

There are two ways to deduct business use of a personal vehicle. You can either take your total business miles driven times the IRS-approved standard mileage rate, or if you use your vehicle more than 50 percent for business, you can deduct your actual costs prorated between personal and business use.

If your vehicle is used 100 percent for business—say it's a utility truck, a dump truck, a delivery vehicle, or a second vehicle devoted to business—and there's no personal use, you must still keep a mileage log.

To determine the business-use percentage for a mixed-use vehicle, divide the business miles by the total miles driven, for example, 7,000 (business miles)/10,000 (total miles) = .70, or 70 percent.

Now that we've established the percentage of business use and the total miles and business miles driven, let's put them to use. You need to determine if you are going to use the IRS standard mileage rate or actual costs.

You cannot use the standard mileage rate if

- your business provides cars for hire (limo service, taxi, etc.);
- you have a business that has five or more vehicles being operated at the same time;
- you are a rural mail carrier who has a qualified reimbursement plan; or

■ you are using an employer-provided vehicle.

If you wish to claim actual expenses, you can deduct gasoline, repairs, and maintenance (don't forget car washes), vehicle registration fees, insurance, tires, car loan interest, lease payments, garage rent, parking, tolls, and of course depreciation, including the Section 179 deduction. Don't forget to deduct the cost of those scented Christmas trees you hang from the rearview mirror.

Fill in the proper boxes on Form 2106 or on page 2 of Schedule C to take the deduction. If you are depreciating your vehicle, include Form 4562, Depreciation. Make sure you keep all documentation concerning this deduction in your tax file in case of audit.

And if you are audited and don't have your paperwork together, don't panic. Let me show you how understanding the folks at the IRS can be. A couple of years ago a new client, Spencer, came to see me. The IRS was in the middle of auditing three years of tax returns and was considering throwing Spencer in jail for tax fraud. And believe me it had a case; the tax returns he filed were as phony as Monopoly money. My firm compiled his books and created proper tax returns and a stay-out-of-jail card.

The auditor disallowed the vehicle deduction because Spencer hadn't maintained a mileage log. I got to work and reconstructed a mileage log based on Spencer's job files and a little help from Mapquest. The results proved his vehicle expense actually exceeded the amount he had claimed. He had likely paid cash for many of his gasoline purchases but had no receipts. I was excited!

But the auditor would not acquiesce. She had the right to deny the deduction because he did not keep a contemporaneous record. I argued that most auditors understand and accept reconstructed records, even reasonable estimates. "Oh c'mon," I said, "He's a contractor. He's got a truck. I mean, duh, he's got vehicle expense. You should allow something. It's only fair."

Finally, the reason for her stubbornness was revealed. The auditor uses her own vehicle and is forced to keep a mileage log so the IRS will reimburse her. And by golly, if she has to keep a log, then everybody else has to. Well, I finally wore her down and she accepted the reconstructed log and 100 percent of the deduction.

I know I have just relieved your mind. However, I'm not going to let you rest easy. Even though my clients and I have had good experiences dealing with the IRS when it comes to vehicle expense, bear in mind that the IRS does not have to accept reconstructed logs. And in our current political climate, when more tax revenues are required to pay for ever-increasing government spending, economic bailouts, wars, and such, the IRS may decide to become stricter. You may find yourself walking out of an audit with a big tax bill because you didn't keep a mileage log.

So go clean your room, quit hitting your sister, and at least mark your annual beginning and ending odometer readings in your appointment book.

Taxpertise Checklist

❑ Mark your January 1 beginning and December 31 ending odometer readings in your appointment book.

❑ Attempt to track business versus personal miles for at least two weeks out of every quarter.

❑ Keep your appointment book with your tax documents in the event of audit.

❑ Keep vehicle repair receipts even if you take the standard mileage deduction; the odometer readings on the receipts will help substantiate the mileage figure on your tax return.

12

Business Meals and Entertainment

Are We Having Fun Yet?

*V*ince has a singing telegram service. When he was audited recently, the focus was on meals and entertainment. The IRS didn't care about the rest of his expenses; it only wanted to see receipts and documentation for those two categories. It's one of the IRS's favorite audit targets simply because most folks don't know the rules.

By the end of the session, Vince owed an additional $28,000 in taxes, penalties, and interest for a three-year period.

What was his downfall? Part of the problem was lack of documentation. Vince had many receipts with no indication of the business purpose or whom he entertained. The story behind other receipts was that no substantial business was conducted; Vince merely said, "They were clients. We went out to have some fun. It was good for business. Whaaaaat? What do you mean it's not deductible?"

However, the major contributing factor to the increase in taxes was the disallowance of one particular entertainment expense. Vince owns a cabin located 50 miles from his home. He proudly showed the auditor detailed records of dates, times, and amounts spent backed up with receipts and even photos to prove that the cabin was used primarily to entertain clients, employees, and other business associates. And hey, every bit of it was true. Vince is the ultimate party animal and he believes the best way to promote business is to do so with a lampshade on his head. And it works for him. He's got a very successful enterprise.

The auditor was impressed with his documentation skills.

Then he gave Vince the bad news. "You cannot deduct an entertainment facility as entertainment expense. You can't buy a yacht or an airplane or a cabin in the woods and write it off as business entertainment."

Vince was floored. "How do those big corporate guys do it?"

The auditor said, "Well, they don't—certainly not as entertainment expense. They might write it off as office expense. Or maybe they set up a small charter business in their dad's name and take the write-off that way. Have you read Grisham's *King of Torts*?" Then he punched a few keys on his computer and handed Vince the bill.

Are you one of the many self-employed businesspeople who feel a little gun-shy about writing off your travel, meals, and entertainment expenses? Or did I just make you gun-shy with Vince's story? You're out there having fun in the name of business and worried that the IRS will not equate those costs to valid tax deductions, correct?

Of all the business activities you perform, travel, meals, and entertainment are preferable to placing an office supply order or writing a check for a subscription to *My Boring Trade* magazine. Oh, the guilt! Work is no longer drudgery when you're enjoying a fabulous dinner while cutting an exciting business deal. Or flying off to Aruba for the annual trade show. What could be better? Writing it off, that's what. And so you do. And so you should.

Fast-forward and drain out the color. There you are in a cubicle opposite a sour-faced IRS agent scowling over your stack of receipts. Maybe it's the guy Vince dealt with. "I don't know about all this," he says. "It looks like you've been having way too much fun."

Oh, the guilt.

Repeat after me: Business travel, meal, and entertainment expenses are valid write-offs.

- Treating a captive audience to a drink or meal during your sales pitch is an excellent way to spend advertising dollars.
- Discussing business over a glass of wine may induce a potential client or employee to sign on.
- Working with a client on a project over a meal that you pay for creates goodwill.
- Providing a free lunch to the mayor at your restaurant's grand opening not because you like him but because you'll get publicity is deductible.

Memorize these answers before you go to an audit. You may not have to use them because IRS auditors know this. But you may need them to dispel the mud pack of guilt that has settled right there in the pit of your stomach.

If you know the rules behind writing off meals and entertainment, you can walk confidently into an audit and watch your numbers fly without a problem.

Let's relieve a little more of that guilt. You have only so many advertising dollars in your budget. There is no law that says you have to spend them in a certain way. Look at how time-share sales are performed. They don't blow a bundle on newspaper or magazine ads. Their strategy is to spend advertising dollars on people and prizes. Telemarketers call to entice you with a free propane barbecue or a two-night, three-day stay at some new development in Maui.

Or how about those living trust attorneys who spend scads on "chicken under questionable gray matter" dinners for seniors while they blather on about asset protection. You'd better believe these costs are written off. And they are valid deductions. Some are classified as advertising, some as outside services, some as gifts. And some of these costs are classified as meals and entertainment expenses, which, by the way, is only 50 percent deductible.

Here are some basic rules:

1. Regardless of whether you put together a seminar for 200 or take 1 potential client to dinner to hear your sales pitch, if your primary intent is to
   - get new business—increase income or derive some other business benefit—or
   - encourage a continuation of an existing business relationship;
2. it takes place in a setting conducive to transacting business, or it occurs in a business setting followed by a fabulous meal or playtime at the local club;
3. there is a substantial business discussion before, during, or after the meal or entertainment; and
4. the meal or entertainment is not lavish or extravagant, it will likely be deductible.

But pay attention: there are many tests, many ifs, ands, and buts. There's a common thread, which you can pick up from the following examples.

- You can take an existing client to a ballgame after a substantial business discussion, possibly as a thank-you for signing that big fat contract. The expense is deductible. But if you said you took him to the game primarily so you could discuss business, it would likely be disallowed because there are too many distractions in such a setting to allow for a serious discussion. You may claim that your expectation was that this setting would be more conducive to a yes answer, but it won't fly.
- You buy a pizza for your staff to keep them in the office working during lunch when you have a pressing deadline. This is definitely

deductible. Business meals and entertainment are normally only 50 percent deductible. But did you know that meals provided to a working crew during business hours for the convenience of the employer are 100 percent deductible? The cost of these meals should be tracked separately from other meals and entertainment so your tax accountant will take the entire deduction rather than apply the 50 percent rule.

■ You spend $50,000 on your daughter's wedding and invite all your clients. NO! That is not deductible. The primary purpose of the event is not to have a serious business discussion. If you believe it is, you need counseling, which, by the way, is deductible.

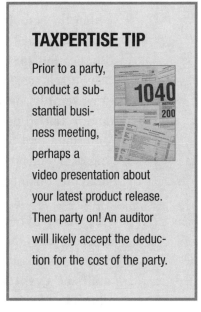

TAXPERTISE TIP

Prior to a party, conduct a substantial business meeting, perhaps a video presentation about your latest product release. Then party on! An auditor will likely accept the deduction for the cost of the party.

■ You have a cocktail party for clients and potential clients. Hmmm. Probably not a write-off because a party is a social occasion, the focus is not business. The focus is getting slammed and dancing on tabletops. This is how the IRS will look at it, anyway, this is how the auditor who looked at Vince's records saw it.

PASSING THE TEST

Besides demonstrating a business purpose, there are several other important rules to follow to ensure that your meals and entertainment expenses stand up to scrutiny.

■ You needn't supply receipts for meals or entertainment that cost less than $75. However, you need some sort of documentation to prove your case. An entry in your appointment book with the location, names of those you entertained, content of the meeting, and the total cost is sufficient. Might as well have kept the receipt, correct?

- Meals and entertainment are only 50 percent deductible. Meals you eat alone are not deductible unless overnight travel is involved. While traveling overnight for business you may deduct either the actual meal expense or the IRS-approved per diem—the standard meal allowance. Rates and charts are available in Publication 463 on the IRS website.

- If you sell meals, entertainment, or use of facilities to the public, for example, or you own a restaurant or nightclub, don't worry about that 50 percent limit. It doesn't apply to you if the meal or entertainment takes place at your establishment. If you're a clothing designer who puts on a fashion show that is a normal activity for your business, that falls under advertising, which is 100 percent deductible.

- You also will not be subject to the 50 percent limit if you pay for a package deal that includes a ticket to a qualified charitable sporting event as long as all the proceeds go to the charity, volunteers staff the event, and the event's main purpose is to benefit the charity.

- The IRS may disallow anything it considers "lavish or extravagant." Does it offer a concise definition for "lavish or extravagant"? Of course not. The best it does is state that the cost must be reasonable. Here we go again with subjective opinion. So it's up to you to convince the auditor that the cost is reasonable.

  Will the auditor consider your income level and necessity to impress? Let's hope so. Let's also remember that we have appeal rights. You can always run to a manager, who hopefully has more exotic tastes and will agree with your propensity for spending. Just try to keep it down a little.

- The business discussion during the meal or entertainment must be substantial. There have been plenty of associates, friends, relatives, and clients who joined me for lunch and discussed everything from love life problems to politics to "Hey, how 'bout them 9ers?" Everything but business. The check arrives. Snickering, they pick it up, and say, "So how's biz?"

I put on my auditor look of disdain, and retort, "That's why I'm not picking up this tab. This meal is not a write-off." Sorry, but saying, "How's biz?" while you're whipping out your Visa card isn't exactly a substantial business discussion.

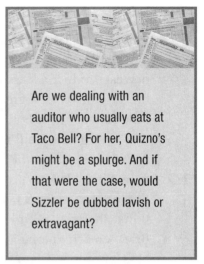

Are we dealing with an auditor who usually eats at Taco Bell? For her, Quizno's might be a splurge. And if that were the case, would Sizzler be dubbed lavish or extravagant?

■ You cannot deduct any "It's my turn to pay" meals. If you dine often with a client, employee, or associate and one time you pay, then the next time he pays, it is not considered a valid and deductible meals or entertainment expense.

■ Business intent as a primary focus during hunting and fishing trips or aboard yachts, pleasure boats, and airplanes is difficult if not impossible to prove in order to validate the expense as deductible. Be prepared to lose the deduction or be armed with substantial proof of primary business intent and content in order to convince the auditor to allow it. Even then, it likely will not fly.

■ Cost of entertainment facilities including mortgage interest, property taxes, depreciation, rent, and so on for swimming pools, bowling alleys, tennis courts, cars, apartments, homes in a vacation resort, and hotel suites are not deductible. Ask Vince. Don't confuse this with occasional use of an entertainment facility. For example, you can certainly deduct the one-week cost of a trade show hospitality suite that shows off your newest products. However, you cannot write off the cost of a yearlong contract for a hotel suite that you use for entertainment purposes or, like Vince, the ownership of a cabin in the woods used primarily for entertaining clients and employees.

■ You cannot deduct dues paid to country clubs, golf and athletic clubs, airline and hotel clubs, and clubs that provide meals while participating in business discussions.

HOME ENTERTAINMENT

Entertaining clients in your home is an area that requires extra documentation. For example, you invite a batch of prospective clients to view your newest product release followed by a sit-down dinner at your house. You hit the store with a grocery list, put it all together, and have a successful little soiree. The IRS auditor rolls his eyes at your $300 receipt and states that your grocery bill is *not* a tax deduction. "But I wrote the check from my business account!" Another eye roll as the auditor disallows the deduction. "It was a dinner party for my clients. There's four pounds of Brie on that receipt. I can't eat that much!" The auditor tells you that he thinks that you, your kids, and a dozen other friends and relatives ate the Brie. A receipt alone is not sufficient proof that the dinner was for business purposes. Sorry, but you're basically doomed. You might get the deduction after arguing it to death with the auditor and possibly his manager. But why not make it easy on yourself?

Here's how to make this dinner deductible without a second glance from the auditor: staple the store receipt to a copy of the dinner invitation (which of course mentions the viewing of the product release or the guest lecturer or whatever business purpose) and the guest list, and possibly a picture of hungry clients diving into said Brie in front of a counter containing your company's newest products.

PROMOTION AND GIFTS

If you're looking for less hassle and a 100 percent write-off versus the 50 percent deduction you're allowed for meals and entertainment, you may want to consider spending your advertising dollars in the area of promotion and gifts rather than meals and entertainment.

What's the difference? Besides getting the full deduction, that is? The main method used to convert 50 percent deductible entertainment or meals expense to 100 percent deductible gift or advertising expense is to make sure you do not attend.

Let's take those time-share salespeople for a moment. If you endure their sales pitch, you automatically get a two-night, three-day stay at a

Maui five-star resort. If the IRS were to look at this expense, it would call it promotion and allow a 100 percent deduction. That's because none of the principals of the time-share company are going along with the lucky couple.

Same principle applies to your business. Maybe you have a contest and the winner gets a trip or a meal for two at a local restaurant. You can classify the expense as promotion and get a 100 percent deduction. If you join them for the meal, the expense is subject to the 50 percent reduction.

Gifts—what a joke. You are allowed a deduction of $25 per year per recipient and that's it. Since this rule was established, way back in the day, the amount has never been adjusted for inflation. Wrapping paper, ribbon, engraving, gift cards, insurance, and mailing are considered incidental costs and not included in the $25 cap.

If the item costs $4 or less and has your company name permanently imprinted on it, it is not considered a gift. It's considered a promotional item and can be listed under advertising expense.

If you give a customer tickets to a theater performance or a sporting event that you do not attend, you have a choice of treating it as a gift or as entertainment, whichever is to your advantage. So if tickets cost $100, you may want to treat it as entertainment because your write-off would be $50 after the 50 percent haircut rather than the maximum of $25 if you were to call it a gift.

Don't think you can double the gift deduction by including your spouse or business partner as giver to the same recipient. Under this definition, you and your spouse or you and your business partners are considered one giver.

Meals and entertainment are a necessary component of the American dream and the pursuit of happiness. If you follow the rules, you can enjoy life and enjoy your business endeavors to the fullest while you stuff extra tax dollars back into your pocket.

Taxpertise Checklist

❑ When planning expenses, decide if the activity is meals or entertainment (50 percent deductible), advertising, promotion (both 100 percent deductible), or gifts (limited to $25 per person per year).

❑ Document receipts with business purpose and name of person entertained.

❑ If you do not have a receipt, document the event, amount, and persons entertained in your appointment book. When you log the information into QuickBooks, transfer the info to the memo line.

❑ Track on-premises employee meals (for the convenience of the employer) separately from other meals and entertainment expenses, as they are 100 percent deductible.

13

Business Travel

Get Me the Hell Out of Here and Let Me Write It Off

*S*usannah rented a four-bedroom cabin in Squaw Valley during ski season one year. But the trip was not for pleasure. She took her six employees, all physical therapists, to stay there for the week while attending a physical therapy convention at a local hotel. They got in only one afternoon of skiing because the convention lasted from 8 A.M. to 5 P.M. every single day, except for the last day, when they adjourned at noon.

When Susannah was audited three years later, the auditor disallowed all $12,000 of the expenses for the trip and presented her with a tax bill for more than $5,000.

Was it because they skied for a few hours? No. That would have actually been fine. It was because Susannah could not come up with a shred of evidence proving that this was a business trip. All she had was a credit card statement with charges for the lodging, meals, skiing, and a few incidentals, none of which proved the trip was business-related. She couldn't prove who was with her. To the auditor it looked as if she had taken a very nice vacation.

"I swear to the most holy of holies that this was a business trip!" she told the auditor.

The auditor flashed her practiced look of disdain and said, "You have to do better than that. You have to prove it."

In the eyes of the IRS, we are all guilty until proven innocent.

Susannah went on an expedition into her storage space. She remembered that she had paid for the conference two months before the trip but could not find the receipt, cancelled check, or credit card charge. The firm who sponsored the conference was now out of business, so there was no one on that end to verify the expense. She searched and searched but found nothing. Susannah wondered if she had paid for it out of her personal account, like she sometimes does. She had thrown away those bank statements.

Susannah didn't want to ask her employees to sign affidavits. First off, she didn't want them to know she was being audited. And secondly, she didn't want them to feel put on the spot. As soon as people know they have to make a statement to the Internal Revenue Service, they tend to disappear into the woodwork. Can you blame them? Susannah worried that if they signed the affidavit, it would be an invitation to the IRS to audit them next. Employee relations were more valuable to her than that. Also, she wasn't sure the auditor would allow the deduction simply because her employees backed her up.

So Susannah lost out on the deduction and paid the additional taxes plus penalties and interest. She felt it was a small price to pay to guarantee employee confidence and happiness. But it was a severe financial lesson in terms of keeping proper records.

And because it was not a no-change audit and because deductions were disallowed and Susannah owed additional taxes for that tax year, the IRS proceeded to look at the other two years that were still open in its audit window. Suspecting that she wrote off other personal expenses, it picked apart every deduction and examined every piece of documentation.

EVIDENCE

Because travel is one of the main categories in which taxpayers are suspected of writing off personal expenses, it is important that you keep every shred of evidence to prove that the primary purpose of the trip was business.

More importantly, learn the rules, so that you deduct all that you are allowed to and don't deduct more than you should. So let's lay down some tracks right now. The rules governing the deductibility of travel are very tricky and complex. Because of this, you may want to double-check with your tax pro to ensure that your travel expenses are deductible.

Ordinary and necessary travel for business is deductible, as long as the *primary* purpose of the trip is business. Travel is defined as being away from your tax home substantially longer than an ordinary day's work.

YOUR TAX HOME

The first thing to do is define your tax home. Your tax home may not necessarily be your personal residence. For most people it is. However, the definition of tax home revolves around where your business is conducted, where most of your income is derived. Most of us live near our job and can easily define our tax home as our personal residence.

Some people do not have a regular or main place of business. If so, you would consider the place where you regularly live as your tax home.

If you still can't decide where your tax home is, here are three factors to consider:

1. you perform part of your business in the area of your main home and stay in that home while you carry on business in the area;
2. you duplicate the living expenses at your main home because your business requires you to be away from that home; and
3. you haven't abandoned the area where your main home is located. Family members may still be residing in the home and you stay there often.

If you don't satisfy these three factors, you may be considered an itinerant with no tax home. That means your travel expenses are not deductible. This would be the case if, say, you're a hit man who is constantly on the road going from one hit to the next, hiding in this hotel and that out-of-the-way dive. Maybe you have a girlfriend in Florida and hang out there every few weeks but don't pay rent. Another dalliance in Dallas provides you with shelter and three squares. Sorry, Mr. Hit Man, but your travel expenses are not deductible.

Once you have established the location of your tax home, you may be able to write off your business travel. But of course, the rules are not clear-cut, not simple at all. Here are a few examples to help illustrate some of the more important rules.

If your personal residence is in New York City and that is where your spouse and kids reside, but you regularly work in Los Angeles, your tax home would be considered Los Angeles. If this were the case, then business travel would have to originate in Los Angeles rather than New York. The cost of flying to the family home in New York to visit the wife and kids would not be deductible. Nor would the amounts paid for lodging and food in Los Angeles be deductible. Ouch.

But if you were flying back to New York for a meeting at corporate headquarters and happened to pop in on the family, the cost might possibly be considered a legitimate business travel expense. It depends upon the facts and circumstances. Was the primary purpose to visit the family or was it to attend the meeting? How much time was spent on each activity? The auditor will play 20 questions with that one.

Same circumstances, but let's say that the job in Los Angeles were merely a temporary assignment—that is, lasting less than one year; your

SOME TRAVEL EXPENSE TIDBITS

Any travel allowance income you receive from a client or your employer must be declared as income on your tax return.

If you travel to acquire a new business, your expenses are startup expenses, not travel expenses, and subject to a completely different set of rules. Check with your tax pro.

If you are looking for a new job in an existing field, the costs are deductible. But if you are looking for a new career, the costs are not deductible.

Travel to investment seminars is not tax-deductible.

Is your head ready to spin off yet?

tax home would be New York. Now you may deduct your living expenses (lodging and food) in Los Angeles as travel expenses. If the temporary assignment turns into a permanent assignment, you may deduct the expenses up to the point where it becomes a permanent assignment. At that point you may want to consider moving expenses as a deduction because that's all you'll have left. Once it's a permanent assignment, Los Angeles becomes your new tax home.

SHORT BUSINESS TRIPS

The most common travel expenses deducted on a tax return pertain to short business trips. Basically, the travel must be primarily for business. It's okay to add on a few hours of skiing or a couple of sightseeing tours. But if it's primarily a vacation and you shoot off a resume to a local business while you're there or you view videotape one afternoon on a business-related subject, then none of the trip is deductible. The business purpose will be considered incidental rather than primary.

However, any business expenses you incur during a personal trip, aside from the travel and lodging, are deductible. For example, if on your one-week vacation to Cabo you take a potential client to lunch to discuss a business deal, the lunch would be a write-off. But the trip to Cabo—the airfare, the lodging, the other meals? Nope, not deductible.

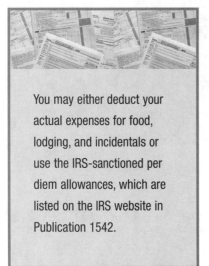

You may either deduct your actual expenses for food, lodging, and incidentals or use the IRS-sanctioned per diem allowances, which are listed on the IRS website in Publication 1542.

Now let's say the trip to Cabo is to attend a three-day, nine-to-five, highly intense trade show where you will be revealing your newest product line. Or it's to have a series of meetings with principals of another company to sell them your product or service. Or it's a trip to pick up continuing education credits to improve or maintain skills in your existing occupation. Make sure that most of your time is spent on a business purpose.

Once you've established a primary business purpose, you can write off the following:

- Transportation, parking and tolls, airport shuttles, taxi
- Shipping of baggage
- Rental car, including operating expenses
- Lodging
- Meals
- Tips and laundry
- Telephone, computer rental, temporary office help
- Any other ordinary and necessary travel expenses and incidental expenses

As with meals and entertainment expense, the "lavish and extravagant" rules apply. Also, remember that meals and entertainment are subject to the 50 percent reduction.

BRINGING COMPANY

You normally cannot deduct expenses for another individual who travels with you. Expenses for a spouse, girlfriend or boyfriend, son, daughter, or best buddy are not deductible. If you take one of these folks, you might pay $170 for the room's double rate. But because your companion does-n't qualify for the business travel deduction, the amount you may write off will be the cost of the room's single rate, say $140.

If you take an employee or business associate, the expenses are deductible if there is a bona fide business purpose for that person's atten-dance or if he would otherwise be allowed to take the deduction himself. And his contribution to the business purpose had better be substantial. For example, you cannot take your hot little secretary because she would be great at helping you entertain the client or you need her to type up a few notes. IRS auditors will not consider her presence necessary to the conduct of business. Neither is the presence of a spouse to help entertain, lend you credibility, improve your image, or ease the tension at the end of the day. Sorry, it won't fly.

But say you need to bring along the company's attorney to explain the intricacies of a big business deal. Without him you will face gridlock in the negotiations. Or you bring along that young maverick negotiator because he has skills that you only wish you had. He will get the job done. Now we're talking a bona fide business purpose. Or you bring along an employee to an educational conference, like our friend Susannah did, to improve his existing job skills or fulfill his continuing education requirements. If this is the main purpose of the trip and most of the time is spent on the business activity, you've got deductible travel expenses.

PROVING IT WASN'T FUN

Don't have too much fun or you'll find those expenses up for scrutiny and likely disallowed. Okay, picture this: You go to a trade show in Maui working from nine to five for three days in the conference center. You hook up with other businesspeople, network, trade business cards, and learn about products and services in your field and in complementary industries. You sell a little and promote your business. You have no time to hit the beach. Even your free time is filled with dining and hobnobbing with colleagues. How pathetic is that?

Three years later you're showing your credit card statements to an IRS auditor, who puckers a condescending scowl and says, "A trade show in Maui? Yeah, right. Sounds like a vacation to me! Disallowed!"

But . . . but . . . but . . . your shoulders droop as you rack your brain trying to figure out ways to prove it was a business trip. Can you tell her how bored you were with the Perkins' presentation? About how you stared jealously out the window at the surfers crashing with the waves on the beach? Will she believe you when you tell her how you went upstairs for a quick nap before a night on the town and didn't wake up until the next morning?

Here's what to do: Keep the fliers advertising the trade show, the business cards you collected, copies of the letters and e-mails you wrote to the folks you met there. Make sure you include "nice discussing this project with you over dinner last night at Sam's" in your correspondence. Store these documents with the credit card statement. Now you've got your proof and you don't have to go look it up anywhere else. It's attached to the document the IRS will require in the event of an audit, the credit card statement. The deductions will be allowed.

I had a client in this situation who not only had proof of the trade show but also had retained a copy of a fax from his boss allowing him to stay over a few extra days to make follow-up sales calls. The auditor allowed the expenses for the Honolulu business trip as well as for the hotel and meals costs of the extended stay.

When a person tacks on personal vacation time to the tail end of a business trip, he cannot deduct the hotel and meals during the personal time. The returning transportation cost is still deductible because, after all, you do have to return. Supposedly.

Taxpertise Checklist

❑ Establish the location of your tax home.

❑ Retain all fliers, correspondence, and any other documents to prove the primary purpose of the travel is business. Store them with your tax return.

❑ If audited for travel expenses, bring every document that will substantiate the business purpose.

Bull and Red Flags

The Sales Tax Return

*Tax Law Written During the
Mad Hatter's Tea Party*

*A*ngie, a graphic artist, came to me one day in a panic. The California State
Board of Equalization had audited her records for the past three years and determined that she owed a whopping $7,000 plus penalties and interest. Angie was
five months pregnant. The tax bill pillaged her nursery budget.

"They are so nitpicky! If you sneeze once, it's taxable. If you sneeze twice, it's
not taxable! I render a service and as far as I knew, services aren't taxable. Now

If you think the IRS complicates things, you haven't even begun to experience the head-exploding tax laws generated by the sales tax agencies of this nation.

all of a sudden I was supposed to be charging sales tax. But not on everything. Some stuff is subject to tax; other stuff isn't. And it depends on this or it depends on that. I don't even know. Unbelievable!"

I pushed a box of tissues across the desk, then reviewed the records and the audit results and felt just as disgusted as Angie. Instead of clear-cut, easy-to-follow principles, the sales tax code is riddled with exceptions and complications. And they hit every industry out there.

It reminds me of a depreciation rule I once read concerning nut trees. Three paragraphs of explanation about how you calculate the deduction. The last paragraph listed the nuts to which the law referred: "This applies to walnuts, hazelnuts, brazil nuts, peanuts . . . blah, blah, blah . . . all nuts in these categories WITH THE EXCEPTION OF ALMONDS"! Oh good grief, another eye-rolling tax law. Are they nuts? What's the matter? Didn't the lobbyists for the almond industry kick down for the tax deduction? Makes you wonder.

Anyway, back to Angie. Poor Angie. The taxability of her work depended upon who owned the copyright. It also depended upon whether or not she added text to any of the graphics she designed. And that wasn't the end of it! I spent 30 minutes groaning and rolling my eyes as I read the report and checked the law.

Luckily, the California State Board of Equalization had published a 47-page brochure to offer guidance specifically for the graphic arts industry. If Angie wanted to be in compliance, she had a lot to memorize. Either that or she would be spending most of her days checking tables and charts to determine if she should collect sales tax on the pen slash she just made.

It would be nice if sales tax regulations were simplified. Make Angie's industry, graphic design, either taxable or not. Real easy, completely clear-cut.

SALES TAX LAW IN DETAIL

Self-employed individuals have it rough enough trying to keep up with payroll tax law, independent contractor classification dos and don'ts, and knowing what they can and can't deduct for their business.

I live in California. Human nature being what it is, I'd be willing to bet that your state taxing agency is just as crazy as mine. Here are a few rules California has laid down that will blow you away:

- If you're an interior designer, the time you spend designing is not subject to sales tax, but the time you spend shopping for your client is.
- If you are a shower door installer who charges a lump sum (combining the cost of the shower door and installation labor as one line item on the invoice to your customer), charge sales tax on your *cost* of the shower door. If you separate labor from parts on the customer's invoice, charge sales tax on the *selling price* of the shower door.
- If you're a graphic artist, sales tax may apply depending upon who owns the copyright of the material you create.
- If you purchase something not for resale, something to use in your business or for personal use without paying sales tax on the purchase, you must pay use tax on that item.

And this is just a sampling. I own a *Master Sales and Use Tax Guide,* published by ADP. It is 1,144 pages long. Yeah. Memorize that. There will be a test. The complexities, exceptions, and rules will drive you crazy. Therefore, it's important to understand the laws that govern your particular industry. Most sales tax agencies publish smaller booklets that provide specialized guidelines for particular industries. Get the one pertaining to your business and read it cover to cover to make sure you understand what is required of you.

After reading the pamphlet, discuss any ambiguities with a representative of the sales tax board and/or your tax pro. Give a specific example of the type of sale you question. Then ask for a written copy of the sales tax code that applies. Keep in mind that even your tax pro, bookkeeper, customer service representative, or an auditor at the sales tax agency can give you erroneous information.

If you are audited, saying, "You guys said otherwise," will not carry any weight. Even if you have a name to back it up. The auditor will merely respond, "Sorry, but she was wrong. You've got to pay."

Do not rely on another business owner in your industry to interpret the tax code for you. Like Angie, he may misunderstand what is taxable and what is not. Or his knowledge may be outdated. I've seen that happen before. "But Joe's got an upholstery shop, too. He told me I don't have to collect sales tax on the nails I pound into a couch. Now the auditor is saying I have to come up with three grand!"

> Sales tax agencies have made business owners honorary tax collectors. Failing to report and pay sales taxes could result in substantial penalties and possibly jail time.

Even if you believe that your selling activities are not subject to sales tax, it would be a good idea to double-check with your state's sales tax agency to make sure.

Most states require collection of sales tax on all tangible personal property. However, some services may be taxable as well. This is especially true if you live in one of the 11 states that are free from state income taxes. After all, revenues must come from other sources, such as higher-than-average property taxes and higher-than-average sales taxes or sales taxes assessed on service sales. An audit could result in a crippling tax bill if you don't know the rules.

TRUST MONIES

Why so strict? Because you are dealing with a "trust" account; the money doesn't belong to you. Sales taxes that you collect from your customers, like payroll taxes withheld from employees' pay, are trust monies that your business is required to turn over to the appropriate taxing agencies. The consequences of nonpayment are therefore more expensive and devastating. If you are in financial trouble but have enough to pay some of a tax bill, make sales tax or payroll tax a priority over personal or corporate income tax liabilities.

ANGIE'S SOLUTION

Finally, here's what happened with Angie: Unfortunately, the auditor was correct and Angie owed $7,000. Most of the invoices that had been subject to sales tax were for a large project Angie had performed for one client, a major corporation. So I calculated the sales tax for each invoice and constructed a bill. On each line of the bill I entered the invoice number, the taxable service from the original invoice, and the amount of sales tax that should have been collected.

Accompanying the bill was a letter, which read:

Dear Customer,

During a recent sales tax audit, it has come to my attention that I failed to collect sales tax on many of the invoices covering taxable services that I provided to your company. According to the State Board of Equalization, any graphic I create that contains text is subject to sales tax. Therefore, these sales to your company were subject to sales tax.

Enclosed is an invoice detailing each invoice number and the sales tax due on the invoice.

I appreciate your remittance of the balance due of $6,478.30.

Thank you for your prompt attention to this matter.

Angie was surprised when I showed her the bill and letter providing recourse. She said, "I thought I had to pay this bill. I didn't know I could collect it back from my customers." At first Angie was reluctant to contact the company for payment. After she read the letter I composed, she felt better about it. What the heck, it was worth a try. After all, it was money *they* owed, that she was passing on to the state. According to the state rules, she had a right to attempt collection from the customer.

Of course, the state will not get involved in any contract dispute. It will not go after the customer. You are the responsible party; therefore you must pay up whether the customer pays you or not.

If her customer put up a fight, Angie could take the company to court to collect. But most likely, she would not. She prefers to maintain good client relations. She would probably take the hit and pay the bill herself. At least now she knew what services are subject to sales tax and would be in compliance from now on.

Angie shot off the letter and invoice. We sat back and crossed our fingers. Sure enough, 60 days later, a check for the full amount arrived in the mail. Angie called me from Baby Mart and it blessed my day to hear the laughter and gratitude in her voice.

USE TAX

What is use tax? If you use your resale license to buy stuff that you aren't going to resell to customers, you are required pay a use tax on the items. Say you're a copy machine dealer who sells and services copiers. You nab a machine from inventory to use in the office. If you didn't pay sales tax when you bought the machine, you must pay it now in the form of use tax. Use tax also applies to the cost of items purchased over the internet, purchased from sources outside your state, or purchased in any other situation in which you did not pay a sales tax.

> The law states that at the point of final sale or destination, the item is subject to sales tax. And if the final destination is your home or office, then the tax must be collected and paid by you.

The use tax serves to equalize the law. After all, anyone with a resale license can purchase goods as though her intent is resale. If the intent is resale, then sales tax will be collected at the point of resale. But if the intent is to use the item personally or within your normal business operation, then there is no point of resale.

I first became acquainted with the use tax many years ago when I lived in San Francisco. It was customary for residents of San Francisco to purchase major assets in the next county where the sales tax rate was lower. Before I ever owned a business and knew anything about the use tax, I purchased a car in Daly City and saved a half percent in sales tax. I didn't realize I was doing anything wrong.

A few years later the California State Board of Equalization sent me a bill for the difference between the tax rates. Not knowing what it was, I threw it away. A month later someone from the Board of Equalization called me and explained that my automobile purchase was subject to the use tax. He said that although the point of sale was Daly City, my address was San Francisco. I was using the vehicle in a higher tax rate county and was subject to the San Francisco rate.

I basically told him to go to hell. That he should collect the monies from the dealership, not from me. I remember saying, "How do I know you're right? How do I know you're even who you say you are? Send me a copy of the code."

He never sent a copy of the code. In fact, I never heard from him again. I'm sure that since it was a small amount, and I was so stubborn, it was cheaper for them to write it off. And now that I know better, I realize that he was right.

Examples of purchases that are subject to use tax:

- A living room suite purchased by an interior designer at cost for her own home without paying sales tax
- Parts purchased by an auto mechanic for resale that he appropriates for his own race car
- A photocopier that an office supply store purchases for resale but retains to use in its administrative office
- Goods you buy over the internet without paying sales tax that are not for resale
- Inventory purchases for your business that you appropriate for personal use

Use tax is normally reported on your sales tax return. There will be a line item on the sales tax return that reads "Items purchased for personal use" or some similar wording. This is where you will list your cost, not the price you would have charged for the item had you resold it. The amount will be included in the total amount of sales that are subject to sales tax.

If you are not required to have a resale license and fill out sales tax returns but purchase items over the internet, out of state, or from any source that does not charge sales tax, you must report the purchase and pay the use tax on your state income tax return. Your tax pro will likely ask you about this. Compile the total of these purchases to provide to your tax pro.

During a sales tax audit, the auditor will ask to see the depreciation schedules from your tax return and the accompanying receipts for all major assets that you purchased for your business. She will also ask about items purchased with your resale license that you did not resell. Why? She is looking for purchases that are subject to use tax. She will compare these purchases with what you report on your sales tax return or your income tax return to ensure that you have paid the corresponding sales or use tax.

TAX-PAID PURCHASES FOR RESALE

By the same token, if you pay sales tax on items that you purchase for resale, then you generally are not required to collect sales tax from your customer. This can be true for the following tax-paid purchases. (Warning: The following examples are provided to describe the basic principles behind the levying of sales tax. Because there are differences in the law from state to state, please check with your state's taxing agency to ensure that you are in compliance.)

- *Capital equipment purchased with the intent of rental to customers*. For example, if your company's sales activity is to set up audiovisual equipment, you likely have an equipment inventory to draw from. If you paid sales tax when you purchased the equipment inventory, you likely will not have to charge sales tax to your customer. If you rent equipment with the intent of re-renting it to your customer and pay sales tax on the rental, you do not have to charge sales tax to the customer.

- *Supplies and materials purchased for use in construction and installation*. If you are a contractor, it is customary for you to purchase lumber, nails, staples, and so on, and pay sales tax at the source. Therefore, you are not required to collect and remit sales taxes from your customer.

A landscape contractor, for example, may have a choice in this matter. Perhaps she purchases plants, trees, and materials such as mulch and fertilizer on a wholesale basis without paying sales tax. If this is the case, then she is required to collect and remit sales taxes from her customer.

Get the picture?

THE BOTTOM LINE

Somewhere along the line, your state government wants the sales tax monies. If you don't pay them when you buy something, you've got to collect them and pay them when you sell it or use it personally. That's pretty much the basic principle no matter in which state you reside (unless you reside in a state that does not levy sales tax).

Each state has its own set of rules. So make sure you learn them, understand them, and abide by them. Then you, too, can leave the Mad Hatter's tea party without a terrible hangover.

Taxpertise Checklist

❑ Get the sales tax booklet that governs your industry and read it.

❑ Review your sales activities to determine what is subject to sales tax.

❑ If you invoice your customers from QuickBooks, make sure each item is correctly set to taxable or nontaxable and the sales tax rate is correct.

Taxpertise Checklist, continued

❏ Track your sales tax on your accounting software and generate sales tax reports from the software to back up the numbers on the sales tax return.

❏ If you are audited and must pay, you may have recourse from your customer(s).

❏ Declare use tax purchases.

Payroll Taxes

Are You Ready to Meet the Grave and Scary Side of the IRS?

*T*axpayers who do not report and pay employment taxes are treated pretty much the way child molesters are treated in prison. The IRS and the state taxing agencies crack down much harder on those who owe payroll taxes than they do on those who owe income taxes. Why, you ask? Because the money you withhold from Susie Q's paycheck is not yours. It belongs to Susie. It's a trust fund for Susie's benefit. It was never yours. To treat it like it belongs to you is a major sin.

Let's say you promise to pay Susie Q ten bucks an hour to work at your doggy day-care center. That ten bucks is hers. When you issue the paycheck, the government steps in and says, "Fine, the money is hers, but we want Susie's taxes off the top." Those include every amount withheld from Susie's check, also known as trust fund taxes. The feds *want* the following:

- federal withholding, which Susie may or may not get refunded when she files her tax return;
- FICA and Medicare tax, which amounts to 7.65 percent of the gross pay, to stash into Susie's Social Security fund, which she will supposedly receive when she's old and gray;
- FICA and Medicare tax, a matching share of 7.65 percent paid by your company; and
- FUTA tax, which is also not withheld from Susie's pay. You've got to kick that down on your own—.8 percent of the first $7,000 in payroll per employee, essentially a maximum of $56 per employee, paid into the federal unemployment fund.

The state also *wants* its cut:

- income tax (unless you reside in one of the 11 states that don't levy an income tax)—this withheld tax may or may not be refunded to her when Susie files her tax return;
- disability insurance premiums, which are usually paid by the employee—check with your state taxing agency to find out if your state requires withholding for disability premiums; and
- SUTA or SUI, or perhaps your state uses a different abbreviation for what you, as the employer, must pay into the state unemployment fund. This tax is not withheld from the employee's pay. If you live in a state that does not levy an income tax, you may still have to file payroll tax returns showing the employee's salaries and wages and the corresponding calculations to determine how much you, the employer, must pay into the state unemployment fund.

If your business resides where city or county employment taxes are collected, you are required to remit those funds as well.

So here's the drill: You create the paycheck, deduct the withholding taxes, and give Susie her little shrivelled-up net pay. Did you notice, in introducing the federal and state tax items, I highlighted the operative word want? The government *wants* you to deposit Susie's tax withholdings and your share of the employer taxes.

Does someone have a gun to your head? No; you still have control. The pen is in your hand. You must write checks to cover these payroll taxes that are so badly wanted. Not only do you have to remit Susie's taxes (remember, this is Susie's money), but you also have to pay the employer's share. It can be very expensive.

The question is, will you do it? If you are operating your business on a shoestring, you might not write those tax checks to the government. Perhaps there's only enough to pay Susie, your rent, and utilities. So what happens? The payroll taxes are neglected. Truth be told, the sense of urgency to pay the IRS is low compared with other, more pressing expenses. I mean, the rent has to be paid or you're out! And the utilities— how embarrassing would that be to have lights and equipment drone to a stop? Better pay the phone bill, too; that's the business's lifeline. How else are bill collectors supposed to get hold of you?

Your personal expenses cry for attention—house payment, rent, groceries, and shoes for the kids. The IRS? Well, that's just some faceless entity that will eventually send a nasty letter.

And it's not like the government knows you are writing a check to Susie. It has no idea if you even have a payroll going this quarter. There's no pressing bill, no demand notice sitting on your desk, no phone call on the 16th from an IRS agent saying, "Hey, you didn't make your payroll tax deposit yesterday." The government is oblivious until your company files the quarterly payroll tax return. If you've been negligent, that's when it all hits the fan.

Your wheels are turning and you think: "I'll pay with the quarterly payroll tax returns." But with each passing month, the liability increases. When it comes time to file the quarterly payroll tax returns and you see the totals, your eyes bug out. It's always a lot more than you anticipated. You haven't set aside a dime, much less the sum on the bottom line.

TAXPERTISE TIP

Hire a payroll service to prepare, report, and remit the payroll taxes automatically from your checking account every payday. Most payroll services can prepare the required workers' compensation reports and some will disburse the required premiums to the insurance company.

In the meantime, more paydays have come and gone. More taxes remain unpaid. You've gotten a bill, then later a reminder of taxes due. Penalties accrue. And these are the stiffest, most expensive penalties levied against any taxpayer—100 percent of the trust fund tax liability. Not only have you neglected your obligation to turn over the taxes, but you have robbed Susie as well. The government figures that's worth more than a wrist slap.

Was Susie really robbed? Does this mean she can't get her tax refund? No, she'll get it if she's due one. Susie will also receive credit in her Social Security account, whether you paid it or not. The IRS will front it all. But it ticks the IRS off to do so. Her withheld taxes are considered a trust fund, which you, as the employer (and honorary tax collector), are required to turn over to the government.

And that's just the IRS. If you owe withheld and employer-paid state and local taxes you may possibly face even more severe consequences. In fact, some states don't have a statute of limitations on collections of payroll taxes. You could owe the liability for the rest of your life.

This is why I advise my clients to go without food in order to comply. Be sure to calculate your anticipated payroll burden—net pay, payroll taxes, and workers' compensation insurance. Prepare for it, save for it, and make it a number-one priority. This is not the bill to let slide! If you have to raise your prices and rates or cut corners on other expenses to cover the additional cost of payroll taxes and insurance, then do so.

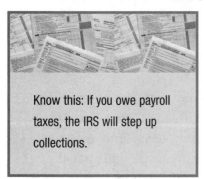

Know this: If you owe payroll taxes, the IRS will step up collections.

When it comes to payroll taxes, the IRS has the ability to make you and your head bookkeeper—actually, anyone who is required to work on payroll—personally liable for the unpaid taxes as well as the 100 percent penalty and interest.

The IRS comes after taxpayers a whole lot faster over payroll taxes than it does if they owe regular income tax liabilities. If the topic is income taxes, the computer will spit out collection notices and letters for six months before the IRS threatens to levy your bank account or other assets. If it's payroll taxes, someone may be knocking at your door in as little as eight weeks.

The IRS will not accept an offer in compromise for trust fund taxes. It's difficult enough getting the IRS to settle for pennies on the dollar for income tax liabilities. But payroll taxes? Forget about it. Even filing bankruptcy won't discharge the obligation.

NEPOTISM

What could be better for a child than to get a real-world education?

If you hire your kid and she is under the age of 18, you are not required to withhold or match the Social Security tax. The wages are not subject to FUTA (federal unemployment tax). But this is only true if your legal form is sole proprietorship. If you do business as a corporation or partnership, you must withhold and pay taxes as though your child were a regular employee.

If you hire your kid to do domestic work, outside of your trade or business, say in your private home, you don't have to withhold taxes or pay the employer share of taxes until the kid is 21.

The nice thing about paying your kids is that you can funnel their pay into an IRA account. If you start early enough, the kid might retire a kazillionaire at age 35.

TAXPERTISE TIP

If you can only make a partial payment of the payroll tax liability, then write a check for the trust fund amount, the amount withheld from your employees' pay. On the memo line, indicate "trust fund taxes" along with your federal ID number and the quarter to which the payment is attributed. By paying at least the trust fund portion, you will avoid the deadly 100 percent penalty.

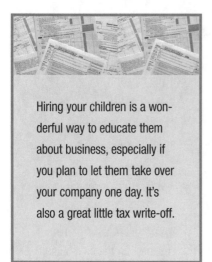

Hiring your children is a wonderful way to educate them about business, especially if you plan to let them take over your company one day. It's also a great little tax write-off.

Make sure you give your child a W-2 at year-end. Deduct his pay on your Schedule C under Wages and Salaries.

You can hire your spouse but you must withhold taxes as though he or she were a regular employee. You don't have to pay into FUTA for your spouse either.

CORPORATE PAYROLL

If your legal form is corporate, you, as the boss, must be on payroll. You cannot take draws like sole proprietors or principals of other unincorporated businesses. If you have an S corporation, you may also take dividends (more about that later) after you have paid yourself a reasonable wage.

Chuck is an attorney incorporated as a subchapter S corporation. The corporate profit was $750,000 last year. Chuck took wages of $50,000 and a dividend of $600,000. The nice thing about taking the profit in the form of a dividend is that you escape payroll taxes. No Social Security or matching Social Security (15.3 percent), no state disability, no state and federal unemployment taxes. The funds are subject only to federal and state income taxes.

This is one of the chief reasons Chuck incorporated his law practice. Nice tax savings, right?

The IRS agrees. In principle. But Chuck's case is a different story. The IRS believes Chuck is abusing the system. The wages Chuck earns are not reasonable. After all, a man of his professional stature and experience would not accept a job at any law firm for $50,000 a year. Even if that law firm offered that amount as a base with profit sharing thrown in, the profit sharing would be subject to payroll taxes. And so, the IRS believes that on a profit of $750,000, perhaps a fairer wage would be $300,000 or more.

So the IRS went back three years and reclassified Chuck's dividends as wages. It zapped the corporation with additional payroll taxes, penalties, and interest.

Chuck wasn't the only attorney to get hit like this. Somewhere along the line, the IRS noticed that this abusive practice was prevalent among lawyers incorporated as S corporations. So a few years ago, the IRS made it a focus of audit and went after attorneys nationwide.

Your business may be new; you may be suffering losses and can't afford to be on payroll. You can't afford to take a dime from the corporation. In fact, you have been lending money to the company. In this case, the IRS doesn't expect payroll expenses.

If you lend money to the corporation, record the loan as a liability on the books. Create a promissory note with a fair market interest rate and set up a repayment plan. Include information about the loan in a board of directors meeting.

> To protect your corporation from audit, be sure to pay yourself a reasonable salary. There are occasions when you can draw funds from your corporation without calling it payroll. But before making any moves, review strategies with your tax pro.

Imagine that time passes and the corporation begins to show a profit. You require funds for personal use, so before going on payroll, you take loan repayments. The nice thing about drawing funds in this fashion is that the only portion of the repayment that is taxable to you is the interest. Of course, the only portion that is deductible to the corporation is the interest. Principal sums invested are not income and principal sums repaid are not deductible.

Nothing wrong with taking loan repayments and going on payroll later. Just make sure you have a sizeable amount of paid-in capital versus loan balance. Do not reduce the initial investment that funded the corporation. Check with your tax pro and attorney before taking action because this can be a tricky situation. There are legal as well as tax implications in how you treat funds invested into the corporation and funds drawn by officers of the corporation.

Another way to draw money from a corporation without a worry of payroll taxes is in the form of rents. Office space in your home or a building you own, your personal vehicle(s), or other equipment can be rented to the corporation at fair market value. Here again it would be wise to consult with a tax professional and attorney to determine what assets should be owned by the corporation and which should be retained personally and rented or leased to the corporation.

I suggest you get Publication 15, *Circular E, Employer's Tax Guide*, and study the different forms of pay including vehicle allowances, fringe benefits, and tips. Circular E discusses the taxability of each category of pay. As an employer, you must acquaint yourself with the full law concerning payroll.

Taxpertise Checklist

❑ Project your payroll costs and make them a budget priority.

❑ Go without food if that's the only way to make your payroll tax deposits in a timely manner.

❑ Consider hiring your children or spouse.

❑ If your legal entity is corporate, pay yourself a reasonable wage. But speak with your attorney and tax pro to determine other legitimate means to draw funds from the corporation.

How About Using Independent Contractors Instead?

Who Qualifies and Who Raises Red Flags

I see your wheels turning. In the previous chapter you saw how expensive it can be to have employees and how terribly expensive it can be if you don't hold up your end of the deal with the IRS and the state. And you're scared. Perhaps you just started your business and you don't think you can afford to put someone on payroll but you really need help. Or maybe you can afford it, but you don't want to deal with the extra expense or paperwork.

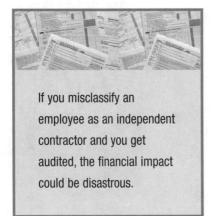

If you misclassify an employee as an independent contractor and you get audited, the financial impact could be disastrous.

Many small-business owners prefer to avoid the hassle of payroll reporting. Besides the extra paperwork, you're required to fork over for workers' compensation insurance, payroll processing fees, fringe benefits, and vacation and sick pay. It just never ends!

You may ask, "Why can't I just pay these guys as independent contractors?" Sometimes you can. But let's look at the obvious stuff first. Your receptionist, a sales clerk in your retail store, a new employee on probation, and most full-time workers (carpenters, administrative workers, etc.) must be paid as employees, not as independent contractors.

If you end up audited, it's usually the state who performs audits to determine whether you've hired independent contractors or employees. The IRS is rarely concerned. I don't know how many income tax audits I've been involved with where the discussion went like this:

> *Auditor:* Got a batch of subs here. Did the taxpayer file any 1099s?
>
> *Me:* Uh, no. (The penalty is $50 for each failure to file.)
>
> *Auditor:* Well, tell him to start filing them, OK?
>
> *Me:* Whew. Okay, by golly, I'll make sure he does.

And that's it. No penalties levied, no studies to determine if the subject should be classified as an employee. Hell, you're already under audit; the IRS usually doesn't kick you while you're down. Climates change, however. One day, I'm sure the IRS will become as diligent as the states. In fact, as of this writing, Congress is considering a federal withholding on all 1099 recipients.

CLASSIFYING THE WORK PROVIDED

So back to the state, who is slaphappily auditing one industry after the other every year in order to collect those extra payroll tax revenues. One of the first things the auditor will look at is whether or not the service performed by the worker is the same service offered by your company.

An example from a recent string of audits: You run a day spa and you hire a masseuse as an independent contractor. The California Employment Development Department (EDD) hit a huge number of wine country day spas and reclassified their on-call masseuses as employees. The severity of the tax bills and penalties put some spas out of business.

EDD's reasoning is that the masseuse offers the same service as the company offers to its clients. It does not matter that this individual works for ten other spas as well as out of her own home studio. It does not matter that she receives a 1099 and files a Schedule C to report the income from all of the spas she services. It doesn't matter that she is licensed by the state and expects to be treated as an independent contractor. It doesn't matter that the masseuse doesn't pull a shift; she merely responds to a request to fulfill a particular appointment at a specified time. Nor does it seem to matter that it is customary in the industry that the smaller spas pay every masseuse on the phone list as an independent contractor.

None of that matters. Spa owners are required to pay the masseuse as an employee primarily because the masseuse provides the same service that the company provides. Other components to EDD's decision include the following:

- The masseuse uses the tools and supplies provided by the spa. There is a room already set up with a massage table, sheets, and a basket of oils and lotions, all of which belong to the spa.
- The masseuse pulled a shift, handling phones and walk-ins, and between appointments she performed other duties around the spa such as laundry, cleaning, and replenishing supplies.

But if a day spa hires a janitor to clean the spa, that individual will likely qualify as an independent contractor. Like the masseuse, the janitor offers her services to a variety of clients, has a business license, and files a Schedule C reporting her 1099 income and expenses.

However, the factor that makes the status of independent contractor acceptable is that the janitor performs a service that is not routinely offered by the clients she services. In other words, the spa is not providing janitorial services.

Let's look at the other rules. The IRS and your state employment department have criteria to determine whether the worker should be classified as an employee or as an independent contractor. Most of it is about control.

Behavioral Control

Do you have the right to direct or control how the work is done through instructions, training, or other means? If so, this guy's an employee.

Financial Control

Financial control covers facts that show whether the business has a right to direct or control the financial and business aspects of the worker's job. This includes

- the extent to which the worker has unreimbursed business expenses;
- the extent of the worker's investment in the facilities used in performing services;
- the extent to which the worker makes his services available to the relevant market;
- how the business pays the worker; and
- the extent to which the worker can realize a profit or incur a loss.

If the worker offers services that are different from what your company offers, has his own business license, sends you an invoice for services performed, and has other clients, then he more than likely will pass the test to be treated as an independent contractor. But there's more.

Type of Relationship

"Type of relationship" covers how the parties perceive their relationship. This includes

- written contracts describing the relationship as that of an independent contractor;

- whether the worker provides services to others;
- whether the independent contractor receives employee-type bene-fits, such as insurance, a pension plan, vacation pay, or sick pay;
- the permanency of the relationship; and
- the extent to which services performed by the worker are a key aspect of the regular business of the company.

For example, if you're a general contractor, and a carpenter works five days a week for only your company, he is defined as an employee. You will have to cough up beaucoup bucks as well as penalties and inter-est if you paid him as a subcontractor.

But say you hire an individual to set up your web page for your wine accessories business. This person has a business license, works for lots of other clients, invoices you on her own company letterhead, and makes you sign a contract. You're definitely looking at a bona fide independent contractor relationship. You've got a written contract saying so, you're not his only client, it's a temporary gig with no fringe benefits attached, and your business does not offer web page design as a service to your clients.

THE OLD UNDER-THE-TABLE ACT

If after all this, you realize that the person you wish to hire should be clas-sified as an employee, you may ask, "How about if I just pay him under the table?"

Please don't go there! Why should you? If you pay someone under the table, you not only lose the deduction, but you will pretty much have the same tax liability as you would if you had placed him on payroll. If you pay him cash, then your self-employment income increases by the amount of the lost deduction, which is subject to regular income tax and self-employment tax at the rate of 15.3 percent. You might save a few bucks in payroll processing fees and payments into the federal and state unemployment funds, but that's certainly not enough to justify the risk.

Why should you, as an employer, pick up the tab on anyone's income taxes by paying her in cash? Why should you risk discovery and then be obligated to fork over payroll taxes, penalties, and interest?

And where's the justice? We have to file our tax returns and pay taxes. So what the hell? Shouldn't the people who work for us have the same responsibility?

Here's a true story of how the state can wreak merciless devastation on a business that does not comply with the law. Darrell operated a telephone installation business. He treated his employees as independent contractors. He didn't see a problem; it seemed like the right thing to do. His 20-some-odd workers had their own tools and their own trucks. But they all worked full time for Darrell, and Darrell alone. Darrell provided them with their daily schedules. None of the workers was required to be licensed. None of them worked for other companies.

Darrell didn't want the hassle of payroll reporting; he wasn't a paperwork kind of guy. To make up for the payroll taxes and increased tax liabilities of his workers, he kicked down a few extra bucks in the hourly rate he paid his guys.

Darrell and his boys worked merrily along, breaking the law day after day. Every January Darrell provided them with Forms 1099. He was sure that he was in compliance. His workers declared their incomes on their tax returns and paid their fair share of taxes.

One day Darrell got angry with Mike, one of his independent contractors, and fired him. Mike marched down to the state and filed for unemployment, listing Darrell as his last employer.

The good folks at the unemployment office told Mike that there was no record that he'd been on payroll at Darrell's company, and therefore, he was not eligible for unemployment. After speaking further with Mike, they realized that Mike did not qualify as an independent contractor and should have been on payroll.

When Mike informed them that Darrell had 20 guys working as independent contractors, the state rubbed its hands together and went after Darrell. After several months of poring over his records, the investigators decided that all 20 independent contractors should have been on payroll. They went back three years and levied employer taxes against Darrell. It added up to quite a sum. The California state unemployment fund charges a variable annual percentage of the first $7,000 of each employee's pay. The rate depends on several factors and varies from employer to employer. For Darrell the rate was 3.4 percent. On 20 guys over a three-year period, this amounted to $14,280. Interest and penalties were added. They also billed him for the disability premiums he should have been withholding from each worker's weekly paycheck. By the time they were finished with him, he owed upwards of $25,000.

It gets bloodier. The unemployment people blew the whistle to the IRS, who came in crouching-tiger-style and levied Darrell for matching FICA tax and FUTA tax for the same three-year period. Damn near a hundred thousand dollars all together. There was no way he could pay it. He was just a middle-class working guy making a halfway decent living. Darrell closed the doors and disappeared.

It would behoove you to make sure you are in compliance. A disgruntled worker can bring you down. An audit can bring you down. It's so much easier when you don't have to look over your shoulder.

If you still have doubts about classification, talk with your accountant or payroll service, or better yet, contact your state employment department. Most states can guide you to a proper determination. I suspect your state will lean heavily toward classifying workers as employees because of the extra payroll tax revenues. But there are forms you can complete and submit for a written determination. If it's in favor of treating a category of worker as an independent contractor, then frame it! Keep it handy. If you are ever audited, you will have proof that this classification has been sanctified. The auditor will have no choice but to pack up his little laptop and take the rest of the day off.

Taxpertise Checklist

- ❑ Obtain a proper determination for treating a worker as an independent contractor rather than an employee.

- ❑ Independent contractors must fill out Form W-9 to provide you with the information needed to issue a Form 1099. Keep the signed W-9 in the worker's file.

- ❑ Send Forms 1099 to all persons who provide services in excess of $600 per year.

- ❑ Study the Form 1099 instructions on the IRS website to ensure that you are in compliance.

Can't They Just Leave Me Alone?

Dealing with Notices from the IRS and Other Literary Tests

Origami Kit Included

*A*l is a very sophisticated businessman with an MBA and years of entrepre-
neurial experience. One day he showed up at my office. In his trembling hands
was a familiar thick envelope. Panic laced his voice as he asked, "What did I do
wrong? Are they auditing me? Do I have to pay something? What is this?"

I kept a straight face, but deep inside I was snickering. I recognized the
envelope, with a big "1040-ES" inscribed below the address block. I knew it

contained blank vouchers for estimated tax payments, something the IRS computer automatically sends to anyone who has to pay estimated taxes. Al's secretary probably intercepted the vouchers in prior years and directed them to the accountant. This was likely the first time he'd encountered such a thing. And it was the first time I saw with my own eyes the fear-invoking and traumatic impact that the IRS has on the citizens of this great nation. It made me mad that the IRS had the power to bring an honest man to his knees.

But deep inside, I was still snickering. I opened the envelope and considered messing with him, teasing that the IRS had discovered his off-shore accounts and now he owed hundreds of thousands on undeclared income; but when I looked up, my heart broke at his despair, and instead I rushed the truth to him.

I doubt if there is a single individual who has not received some form of correspondence from the IRS. And even if it's something as benign as a stack of useful forms, it inspires dread and anxiety. But if it's something other than that, you may need translation services from Confusem Legalese to basic English in order to figure out what the problem is.

I once received a letter from the IRS disallowing several of my business expenses, including office supplies. I turned to Steve, one of my employees, and said, "Yeah, right, like I'm running a tax service without paper clips." So I called the IRS to ask if they were crazy.

The reply stunned me: "That's just our way of inviting you to an audit."

"But it doesn't say anything about an audit in this letter!"

"How is next Tuesday at ten?"

And so began my familiarity with the IRS's roundabout way of doing things.

THE IRS WAY

Know this: If the letter you receive from the IRS pertains to the collection of a tax liability, there is probably not a human being working your account, trying to pinpoint your assets or seeking government adoption of your firstborn. Yet. A big whirring computer generates all of the collection efforts during the first six months after the tax is assessed. Even after that point, it often takes years before a revenue officer is assigned to the case, if at all. In fact, if you take care of business immediately and are cooperative, you will likely only send correspondence to the big whirring computer or deal momentarily with a customer service representative over the phone.

On any correspondence you receive, there will normally be a contact phone number on the top right corner of the letter. But wait; don't just pick up the phone and call. If you've had any experience with the IRS whatsoever, then you know this will involve indefinite hold time. Take a few minutes to read the letter and find out exactly what the IRS is looking for. You may not need to waste precious time on the phone.

Find out which tax form and tax year the IRS is referring to. If you are self-employed, you likely file more than one tax return. If you have payroll, there are quarterly and annual payroll tax returns. If your legal entity is other than a sole proprietorship, you file a separate income tax return. The IRS may be corresponding about payroll, corporate (partnership, LLC, etc.), or individual tax problems. Listed below the phone number will be the tax form in question:

- 1040, 1040A, 1040EZ—individual income tax return
- 1120, 1120S—corporate income tax return
- 1065—partnership income tax return
- 990—nonprofit income tax return
- 990PF—private foundation income tax return
- 941—quarterly payroll tax return
- 940—annual payroll tax return (FUTA-federal unemployment fund taxes)

The address block will also tip you off. Is the notice addressed to you individually or to your company or to both?

Below the tax form, the tax year is listed. Because it's possible that some entities have a fiscal year-end—that is, a year that ends on a date other than December 31—you will find the entire date spelled out. If it's not listed below the form number, it will be listed just above the indented block on page one that shows how much you owe.

The body of the letter may be long and sound like gibberish to you. But read through it. You will eventually stumble upon what they want from you.

DISCREPANCIES

One of the most common letters sent by the IRS pertains to a discrepancy between what it has credited to your tax bill and what you list as estimated tax payments on your tax return. This letter is called a CP23 (see top left) and the header will proclaim: "We changed your account."

You may have listed $10,000 in tax payments on your tax return but the IRS's research shows only $8,000 was paid in. If you thumb through the letter a few pages, you will find a listing and dates of the tax payments the government has recorded. Compare this with your records to see if it is correct. You may discover that you do in fact owe the money. If so, pay the bill and be thankful you didn't have to spend two and a half hours on hold.

It could be that one of the payments had cleared your bank but was not credited as a payment by the IRS for that tax year. In this case, the IRS is confused. Perhaps the IRS applied the payment to another tax period or perhaps it didn't receive the money at all. A photocopy of the front and back of the cancelled check and an inquiry letter with a copy of the notice may solve the problem. However, I would suggest a phone call to wrangle with them if they did in fact apply it to another year, especially if you specified the year in question on the memo line of the check. If you did not, the IRS has a right to apply it to oldest liabilities first.

But if you mailed the check with the estimate voucher and especially if you inscribed the proper data on the memo line, you have the right to have the payment applied to the specified tax period. You will need to submit a copy of the check to prove it.

Sometimes the taxpayer is confused. When a taxpayer gathers his tax data to prepare his tax return, he may assign the fourth installment of his estimated tax payments to the wrong tax year.

For any given year, the due dates of the four estimated tax payments overlap into the subsequent year: April 15, June 15, September 15, and (here's the overlap) January 15. What may happen is that a taxpayer will mistakenly call the final installment due on January 15 an estimated payment for the subsequent year. For example, the final installment of 2009 estimated taxes is due January 15, 2010. The IRS will credit this payment to 2009. But the taxpayer, when preparing his 2010 tax return a year and a half later, may list this payment for 2010 because it was paid in 2010. It's an error that happens all the time, and it will cause the IRS computer to kick out the "We changed your account" notice.

If your research reveals that's what happened, then you don't need to waste any time on the phone with the IRS. Just pay the damn bill.

Otherwise, call the number indicated. Put on speakerphone and play spider solitaire during your two-hour hold time. Have a copy of your cancelled check handy. You may get lucky. The IRS agent may allow you to fax the check copy to him to resolve the problem. If the person helping you refuses to change the application of the payment, ask for the manager.

> ## TAXPERTISE TIP
>
> In order to avoid confusion, add to the memo line of your check the installment number and year for which the payment applies: "Q4 20___." Make sure your Social Security number and "Form 1040-ES" is also inscribed on the memo line.

OVERPAYMENT

The same notice could be generated to give you credit for taxes you paid but failed to list. This will result in an overpayment, which the IRS will refund to you unless you owe other taxes. It will refuse to refund the money and instead pass it on to other agencies if you owe child support, student loan payments, state income taxes, motor vehicle fees, or Social Security repayments. And of course, if you owe the IRS for prior-year taxes, it will keep the refund and apply it to that liability.

Keep this notice in your tax file to refer to if you don't receive the check.

NEGLECTED ITEMS

Another notice you may receive is a CP-2000. This is also a "We changed your account" notice, but it pertains to items of income you neglected to include on your tax return. The IRS receives third-party reporting documents every year. These are usually in the form of W-2s, K-1s, and 1099s showing how much income you received in wages, partnership or S corporation income, interest, dividends, sale of stocks, sale of real estate, nonemployee compensation, gambling winnings, pension benefits, Social Security benefits, and on and on. When your tax return is processed, the items you list are matched to the1099s generated by the folks who gave you the money.

The IRS recalculates your tax liability based on missing information on your tax return and lists the amount due, which may or may not include penalties but will definitely include interest.

This particular letter runs approximately 12 pages long. You will have to dig deep to find how the IRS came up with the extra balance due. There are several pages explaining the interest formula, a description of the penalties, and your rights as a taxpayer. Somewhere around page 8 you will find your answer. In a blocked-in and shaded area will be a listing of the payer and the amount of income credited to you that the IRS did not find on your tax return. The following page will reveal the calculations used to determine the balance owing.

If the information is valid, there is nothing to do but pay the bill. If you can't pay the whole thing at one time, send what you can. If you are able to pay it off in a few installments over several months, don't bother setting up

TAXPERTISE TIP

If you need more than six months to pay off a tax liability, call the IRS to let it know you are applying for an installment agreement.

an installment agreement; the IRS will charge you for that. Simply make the payments. You will receive follow-up letters billing you for the remaining balance along with additional interest. Don't panic. Pretend the letters are coming from your credit card company. Remember, no demon-possessed individual is working overtime to take away your house, your right arm, and your firstborn child. Not yet anyway. If you can pay off the balance owing in a short period of time, you have no worries.

If you need to apply for an installment agreement, complete Form 9465, Request for Installment Agreement, and submit it with a copy of the notice. If possible, fax it to the person you are speaking with on the phone and ask her to put a hold on collection activity until the payment plan is set up. Make sure you get the person's name and ID number. Document all telephone conversations.

If the information listed in the letter is wrong, you can thumb through the letter to find a form to fill out in which you disagree with the IRS's findings. Fill it out, make a copy for your file, and send it in. If you believe the 1099 is an error, contact the payer by phone and follow up in writing to request that he correct the 1099. The only way the IRS will reverse this tax liability is if it receives a corrected 1099 from the payer. Saying, "Na-hunh, wasn't me," a hundred times won't do the trick. Remember, when it comes to the IRS, you are guilty until proven innocent.

If the information is correct but only part of the amount is taxable, file an amended income tax return. Check the box at the top of the amended return that asks if you are responding to a notice. Include a copy of the notice with the amended return. An example of a nontaxable or partially taxable transaction is if you receive a 1099-B from a stock sale but fail to include the information on your tax return. The IRS will calculate taxes based on the full amount the brokerage firm reports to it. However, the full amount is usually not taxable. After all, you can deduct what you paid for the stock plus commissions paid on both ends of the transaction. The profit, not the proceeds from the sale, is the basis for determining how much tax you owe. If you have a loss on the stock sale, instead of paying extra, you might be entitled to a refund. So file the amended tax return and do so immediately.

Here's a good example: Perhaps you bought 100 shares of stock for $5,000. You sold them two years later for $3,000. You took a loss and repressed the memory, so you failed to report it on your tax return. The IRS will send you a tax bill based on $3,000 of income. Guess what? The IRS actually owes you money, not the other way around. You have a loss of $2,000 ($3,000 to $5,000), which you can deduct against other income on your tax return. Send the IRS a letter thanking it for the reminder, then file an amended tax return and claim your refund.

What has become common in the past several years is the generation of a CP-2000 for amounts that have already been reported on the income tax return. The IRS did not know where to look. You probably included the total from Form 1099-Misc, Nonemployee Compensation, on Schedule C, but the IRS is looking for it on page 1 of the 1040 under "Other Income." It doesn't see it there, so the IRS bills you. This will require a special response:

> Dear Sir:
>
> I am in receipt of your Form CP-2000 for the tax year 20__ (copy enclosed). Please note that the amount of $10,000 on Form 1099-Misc paid to me by Acme Dynamite was included on line 1 of my Schedule C (copy enclosed).
>
> Please reverse the tax balance you calculated and change your records accordingly.
>
> Thank you for your consideration in this matter.

In the "RE:" section between the IRS address block and the salutation, include the tax form, tax year, and your Social Security number. Be sure to include a copy of the notice you received as well as a copy of your Schedule C highlighting the income figure on line 1.

Aside from audit notification, the one piece of mail that sends a shock wave through the hearts of taxpayers is the "Notice of Intent to Levy." Or worse, "Urgent Notice, We Intend to Levy on Certain Assets." Yikes. This means you've been ignoring your tax problems for way too long. But the computer is still performing collection efforts and you've got some time. In fact, the notice will tell you exactly how much time you have. And it won't be much! It's time for you to respond—immediately!

Don't be scared to talk to people at the IRS. They cannot reach through the phone and strangle you. I promise. Okay, maybe they can, but they won't.

Don't respond in writing. It takes them months to process and respond to your correspondence. By then they will have levied your bank accounts, put a lien on your house, or garnished your wages.

Gather your financial information, then pick up the phone and make that call. You may need to file a tax return, make payment arrangements (Form 9465), prepare an offer in compromise, or file financial statements (Form 433-A and/or Form 433-B) to prove that you are uncollectable. Ask them to put a hold on collection activity until you can take care of business. They will generally give you 30 days.

Most of the time, the service rep you speak with will be able to set up the installment agreement or fill in the financial statement forms during the phone conversation. This is why you want to have your financial information handy. She'll ask who you bank with, whom you make the car payment to, whom the mortgage holder is. Don't be afraid to provide the information. They can get hold of it pretty much anytime they need it anyway. So divulge to your heart's content. If you cooperate with the IRS, it will cooperate with you.

If you intend to pay, do so now. The rep can usually take a credit or debit card payment over the phone. I'd prefer to owe the credit card company than owe the IRS. The repayment is cheaper and the consequences of missing a payment are far less severe.

After the IRS agent takes down the information she will put a hold on collection activity during the processing time. Because installment agreement requests seem to get lost in the shuffle quite often, be sure you follow up.

Taxpertise Checklist

❑ Carefully read the notice to determine what the IRS is asking of you.

❑ Prepare your proof and financial information before you call the IRS.

❑ Ask for a 30-day hold on collection activity while the IRS processes any additional forms you must file (missing tax returns, proof of payment, request for installment agreement, etc.).

❑ Follow up to ensure that the IRS received all required documentation and you have reached a satisfactory resolution.

Audits

How to Stay Out of Jail

*T*he IRS will never tell you why a particular tax return is under audit. However, there are certain factors that make it obvious why a tax return was selected.

WHAT TRIGGERS AN AUDIT?

Following is a comprehensive list of things that can trigger an IRS audit:

■ *Failure to include income that has been reported to the Internal Revenue Service. During the month of January, you receive tax documents in the*

PART V ■ CAN'T THEY JUST LEAVE ME ALONE?

mail declaring income and certain expenses that relate to your tax return. For example:

- 1099-INT declaring the amount of interest income you've received from various sources including banks and investment companies
- 1099-DIV declaring the amount of dividends you have been paid on your investments
- 1099-MISC for work as an independent contractor and for rental income from tenants of your commercial properties
- W-2s and K-1s

The Internal Revenue Service receives this same information. When you file your tax return, the IRS plays a matching game to ensure that you have declared all of this income on your tax return. If you have not, the IRS will recalculate your tax liability and bill you accordingly. Also considered an audit, it's basically a by-mail correction notice that is open to dispute.

■ Severe departure from the national standards. The IRS has a construction of tables, available on its website at irs.gov, that indicate by income level and if self-employed, by industry, an average of deductions taken in any given tax year. If your numbers are significantly different than the national averages, you may find your tax return up for scrutiny. Red flags include vehicle expense; charitable contributions, especially noncash ones; meals, entertainment, and travel; and excessively high cost of goods sold.

■ Dramatic change in income and expenses from one year to the next. You may experience a financial downturn that throws you into a loss situation. The IRS may audit just because it is interested in what happened and whether or not you are hiding income. Or if your income suddenly increases, the IRS may be suspicious that you cheated in the past and are now coming clean.

■ Lifestyle audits are supposedly a thing of the past. But come on, you know that lifestyle comes into play. I mean, if you are living in a Beverly Hills mansion, with mortgage interest of $200,000 per year, paying DMV fees on a Ferrari, and making charitable

190   TAXPERTISE

contributions of $50,000 each year, then your tax return had better show more than $36,000 of wages from Oil Changers, right? These incongruities will flag your tax return for audit.

■ Specific industry audits are a continuing IRS project. Every year the IRS selects a particular industry to audit. In recent history it has selected wage earners with a small Schedule C business (looking to blow hobby losses out of the water), attorneys incorporated as S corporations (looking at unreasonable compensation in order to add payroll tax liabilities), and trusts with offshore holdings (looking for tax fraud and unreported income).

WHAT IF I DON'T HAVE RECORDS?

If you are audited and are coming up short on records to prove your deductions, try to get copies of receipts from vendors and bank statements to prove your case. Photos will help if your home office or asset acquisitions are in question.

Sometimes, the record you are supposed to keep is one you create yourself, like a mileage log or tip records. That's what happened to Natalie and 28 of her co-workers.

One year, the IRS selected restaurant servers as audit targets and created a formula to determine unreported tips. The cousin of one of my employees rushed into my office in near hysterics. "I can't possibly owe this much!" Natalie cried as she shoved a tax bill for $3,000 across my desk.

I studied the audit notice (bill), which basically backed into an amount of unreported tip income and levied taxes on a wild guess. I looked at Natalie. "Do you have tip records for this year?"

"Huh?"

"You know, a journal of how much in tips you got every day?" Blank stare. "Tips are taxable income; you know that, right?"

"Well, yeah, but I thought that was part of my W-2."

"The part that's on the W-2 is what the boss knows about—like if someone uses a charge card, the tip is written in. The boss sees the tip and adds it to your paycheck and deducts taxes against it, right?" I asked.

"Yeah. I guess so."

"But if someone gives you cash, you shove it in your apron and your boss doesn't know how much you got, right?" She nodded. "So it never gets on your paycheck. It never gets taxed."

Natalie's face was beet red and she looked ready to cry.

"You're supposed to fill out a Form 4137 and attach it to your tax return so you can pay your taxes on the tips that don't get reported to your boss. Did you do that?"

"No." Natalie's lip quivered and she swiped angrily at a tear escaping the corner of her eye. "So do I have to pay this bill?"

"Hell, no. Not yet anyway. Their formula sucks." And it did. With the amount of unreported income the IRS came up with, you would think these kids were neurosurgeons.

I added, "But it will be a challenge because you're supposed to keep records. If you don't have records to support your income, they can pretty much do what they want. You will have to pay something because you never declared those cash tips on your tax return. It's just a matter of figuring out how much."

I created a more accurate formula derived from sales and other figures provided by the restaurant. Natalie loved it because, if accepted, the IRS would slash her tax bill by two-thirds, from $3,000 to about $900.

I ended up with 29 clients from the same restaurant. I applied the formula to each situation with pretty much the same result: a two-thirds reduction in the tax bill.

But when I arrived at the IRS office in Oakland, the auditor refused to entertain the idea of my new formula. She told me, "We've studied this topic and created what we consider a fair formula." She then advised me to come up with contemporaneous tip records to defend the numbers (or lack thereof) on the tax returns. Impossible. Only one of my clients had kept records.

I wasn't quite at a dead end. My only hope was to move the cases out of Oakland to another auditor who would hopefully be more empathetic, not to mention reasonable. The taxpayer has the right to have his case heard in his home district. And my taxpayers' home district was San Mateo, not Oakland.

In San Mateo, I found an auditor who understood that many of these servers (all of them were in their early 20s) did not bother with such mundanity as keeping tip records. Especially at that age! Aside from youthful ignorance of IRS requirements, there were parties to go to and drinking to be done!

She was happy to give them a break on the record-keeping requirement. She also readily accepted my formula and used it as the standard from that point forward. Talk about a bunch of happy kids. Some of them had been looking at bills totaling $10,000.

The point is, if you don't have records, defend your stance with reason or a reasonable formula. This line of thinking will hold forth on issues such as tips, meals, and vehicle expense.

But why do it the hard way? Retain records to prove every tax deduction and to defend every item of income on your tax return. And don't forget, a picture is worth a thousand words. Keep photos of home improvements, vehicles, and other assets used in your business.

Taxpertise Checklist

❑ Check the national standards at irs.gov to see if your tax return has any red flags.

❑ Keep every document that substantiates the deductions you take and the income you declare with your tax return in the event of audit.

❑ If you are missing records develop a strategy, a formula. Use photos, spreadsheets, and reasoning to convince an auditor that you are entitled to the deduction.

Invited to an IRS Audit?

Don't Go! Send a Pro (or Go Well Armed)

You need never speak to an IRS agent, about any issue, except to say, "My tax advisor is handling this. Here's her number. Please call her." And that will be the end of it.

The IRS agent will respect your wishes and will address all issues with your tax advisor. To make an arrangement in which you do not have to speak to an IRS agent, sign Form 2848, Power of Attorney, assigning the duties to your tax pro.

Despite what you might think, this does not diminish your innocence in the agent's eyes. Whenever I represent a client in audit before the IRS, I do not allow my client to attend.

GOING IT ALONE—NOT

Ah, but wouldn't you like to be a fly on the wall during an IRS audit? Or perhaps you have the confidence to represent yourself and want to see what's involved firsthand. I do not recommend that course of action. You've heard the old adage "An attorney should never be his own client, right?"

Check these personal guidelines to determine if you are intellectually and emotionally equipped to handle the audit process alone:

- *What does your gut tell you?* Are you cringing at the thought of facing an auditor? Are you scared, nervous? Afraid you'll talk too much, with your mouth full . . . of foot? Then don't go; send a pro.
- *How complex is your tax return?* Do you understand the tax law behind every deduction you have taken? If you're a wage earner with a W-2 and some itemized deductions, then go ahead, as long as you understand the tax code as it applies to your tax return.
- *If you are self-employed with a complex income tax return, then don't go; send a pro.* Or go, but if it all goes south, stop the audit. Find a tax pro who can help you, and reschedule.

If you decide to represent yourself, it's important that you understand tax law. Here's why: I recently represented a client in an audit. He's self-employed and on December 29 of the year in question, he purchased a truck used 100 percent for business. He elected Section 179 and expensed $25,000 of the $31,000 purchase price, then depreciated the remainder over five years.

The auditor said, "I will allow the $25,000 max on the Section 179, but I am disallowing first-year depreciation on the truck."

"What are you talking about?" I said. "Of course he gets first-year depreciation."

She placed an IRS publication in front of me and pointed out a code section that seemed to confirm her stance. "The maximum expense deduction is $25,000," she stated.

Well, duh. "Yes. It is," I agreed. "But that's the expense deduction. Depreciation is a whole different animal. You subtract that $25,000 from the purchase price, and that leaves $6,000 that he is allowed to write off over five years, starting with the year in which he purchased the vehicle."

She disagreed.

I said, "So what are you saying? That every tax software program in America is messed up? Is wrong? Because whenever I enter an asset into my top-of-the-line program and take Section 179, it always, without fail, calculates first-year depreciation as well."

Her eyes grew big and she summoned two senior auditors, who agreed with me and told her to allow the deduction. Even IRS auditors learn something new every day.

So are you scratching your head, saying, "What the hell was that all about? You lost me, like, six paragraphs ago. I thought this was going to be an easy book to read?"

If I just lost you, and you are self-employed with advanced tax topics like home office and vehicle depreciation, then you should send a professional. It can get pretty tricky in there.

Of course, there's a middle ground between go and don't go. If you feel confident about your numbers, you might want to defend yourself.

But if at any time during the audit you feel blindsided or dazed and confused, just say so and cut the audit short. You can reschedule a time to send in the big guns.

If you want someone to represent you while you stay at home throwing up, and you don't already have a tax advisor (shame on you) or your

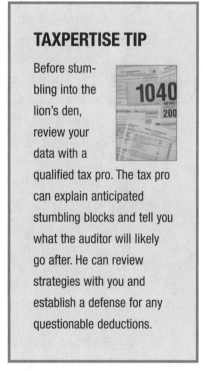

TAXPERTISE TIP

Before stumbling into the lion's den, review your data with a qualified tax pro. The tax pro can explain anticipated stumbling blocks and tell you what the auditor will likely go after. He can review strategies with you and establish a defense for any questionable deductions.

tax advisor isn't cut out for aggressive audit action, ask friends, business associates, and relatives for a referral. You want somebody who sees your side of things, especially if you feel justified in taking a particular deduction that you are worried about. Or maybe he'll just tell you that you're screwed and it's time to move to Mexico. The time to work it out is prior to the meeting with the auditor.

A good tax pro loves to be a hero. She will prepare a hidden arsenal of ammo—overlooked deductions, errors made on the tax return in your favor, and so on. I've whipped those out at the last minute after winning negotiations over subjective areas. "Oh and by the way, the client forgot to deduct expenses for roof repairs on his rental property . . . . How much did you say his refund would be?"

An IRS auditor once told me that most accountants "roll over" during an audit. The auditor disallows what may be a valid deduction (given the right facts and circumstances). The tax pro says OK, scratches his head, rolls over, and then goes on to the next item. Whoa! Don't you want to argue about that a little bit? Make sure your tax pro is willing to go to bat for you.

AUDIT SPEAK

Speaking of subjective areas, here are five phrases that can be used to your advantage during an audit:

1. Ordinary and necessary
2. Not lavish or extravagant
3. Reasonable
4. Business intent
5. Reasonable cause

Take what you learned earlier in the chapters on business income and deductions. Apply these terms and use them when describing deductions you feel should be allowed. Auditors love these familiar buzzwords. They have a soothing and convincing effect. If the auditor wants to disallow a meal you had with an associate, you can say, "Oh my goodness, why would you disallow that? The substantial business

TAXPERTISE TIP

The best time to prepare for an audit is during the year preceding the preparation of your income tax return. Store your bank statements, investment account statements, appointment book, vehicle repair bills (even if you take mileage and not actual expenses; odometer readings on a repair bill will support the deduction), and all other documents relating to your financial transactions with the copy of your tax return. When you gather your tax data to prepare your tax return, examine it as though you are preparing to defend yourself in audit. Add pictures and any other documents you feel are necessary to substantiate any deduction you are prepared to take. Then when and if you are audited, you'll be well armed.

discussion we had at lunch that day was absolutely necessary to keeping his business!"

AUDIT ANALYSIS

When you receive the audit notice, read it carefully. Is it a full-blown audit in which every line item will be examined? Or does the IRS want documentation for only certain entries? Prepare accordingly and bring all requested documents with you—nothing more and nothing less.

If you are invited to an office audit, the auditor is normally allowed three to four hours to review your data to determine if there is a deficiency. You may have heard stories of people dumping a box of receipts, useful and useless, on the auditor's desk with a smart remark like "Figure it out!" Well, I don't recommend that approach. It's easier to catch flies with honey than vinegar. Organize your data by stapling adding machine tapes to the receipts and cancelled checks that match the total for the deduction you took on the tax return. If you performed this task when you prepared the income tax return, you are ready to go.

One of the first things an auditor will examine is your income. He will add up your bank deposits for the year from all bank accounts and match the sum to the income declared on your income tax return. If your bank deposits are greater than the income on your tax return, the auditor will want proof that the additional income was from a nontaxable source, such as fund transfers from another account, loans, credit card cash advances, or gifts.

What does this tell you about audit-proofing your tax return? Make a regular habit of marking bank statements to identify unusual deposits. Attach proof (a copy of the check Mom gave you for Christmas) to the bank statement in the event of an audit. Or mark the business checking account statement with a note next to a deposit, like "from personal savings." It will be easy to identify and prove the deposit was not unreported taxable sales.

Deductions will be examined next. Most of the itemized deductions on Schedule A are straightforward and can be easily substantiated. These include mortgage interest, property taxes, DMV fees, medical expenses, tax preparation fees, and so forth.

If you deduct employee business expenses, those may be more closely examined. What the auditor is looking for is whether or not the expense has been reimbursed and the validity of the deduction. Is it ordinary and necessary? This is why it is important to keep good records.

If you're a nurse and you made an unreimbursed business trip to Las Vegas for a seminar on lactation techniques, then you'd better have the seminar materials and fliers advertising the course as part of your tax file. If all the auditor sees is a credit card charge for the MGM Grand Hotel for three nights, she will likely disallow the expense as personal rather than business. But if you show her a seminar schedule that coincides with the dates of the hotel stay, the expense will be allowed without question.

If you are self-employed filing Schedule C, be prepared to substantiate income and expenses. The auditor will perform the income test on your business checking account to verify that the total of the deposits matches the total sales on line 1. If they do not match, she will want to know the source of the income not reported to determine if it is taxable or not. Just as with your personal checking account, track all sources of nontaxable income so that you will have ready answers when your bank deposits are scrutinized.

The auditor will also examine a sampling of business expense receipts to determine accuracy as well as to determine if the expenses are ordinary and necessary for your type of business.

If you use QuickBooks, print out the general ledger account for the expenses the auditor will review. Here's how to get a report for each expense category under audit:

1. Click on Reports, Company and Financial, Profit and Loss Standard; indicate the dates for the audit period.
2. Go to the line item for the expense in question, e.g., Office Supplies.
3. Double click on the amount listed beside Office Supplies.
4. A transaction detail report will appear showing each transaction by date, check number, and amount paid.
5. Print out the report. Make sure the total matches what is shown on the tax return.
6. Pull the checks, credit card statements, and cash receipts for each transaction and staple them to the printout.

The auditor will like you very much for presenting the information to her efficiently. And like I told you before, it's easier to catch flies with honey.

Part of the $300 billion tax gap that the government complains about is attributed to business owners who attempt to write off personal expenses as business deductions. Auditors are automatically on alert for such transgressions. And the main places they look for them are in areas of travel, meals, and entertainment.

If an auditor reviews credit card statements listing charges for office supply stores, he will rarely request the original receipts. He won't peruse each receipt and ask, "So, these staples you bought . . . you didn't by any chance staple together pages from a letter from your sister, did you? Hmmm? Could be some personal use here. Wonder if I should disallow part of this deduction?" He'll look at the statement, see a charge for 80 bucks from Office Max, and assume it is a business expense without checking each line item on the receipt.

But if you show the auditor a cancelled check for Costco or any store where groceries or other personal items may also be purchased, he will likely ask for the receipt. He will then question the purchase of that 12-pound leg of lamb or the *Tina Turner Sixth Annual Final, Yes, This Is Really the Final Farewell Tour* CD. If these items were personal expenses and you wrote them off, the auditor will view you as a Big Fat Cheater. This will spur him on to dig deep into all of your affairs, because after all, if you're going to write off the family groceries or your personal listening pleasures, then you will probably attempt to write off scads of other personal expenses as well.

It's important to end with a no-change audit, in which you don't incur an additional tax liability. A no-change audit will encourage an auditor to skip examination of any other years that are still open for review. Not only will you save money, which is pretty much the whole point, but you will also likely escape further scrutiny. If the auditor determines that you owe for the year in question, she may want to audit the other two open years as well.

Your tax return will be treated with more credibility if it has been prepared professionally. If you are self-employed and retain the services of a bookkeeper and use a computerized system such as QuickBooks, you may escape closer scrutiny. In fact, more than once, after a cursory review and a sampling of documentation, an auditor has told me, "Well, since your firm prepared the books and you're an Enrolled Agent, I'm not going to dig any deeper. It looks like everything is in order." If a professional prepared your books, let the auditor know.

Don't be afraid to challenge an auditor. Remember the auditor mentioned earlier? The one who was wrong about application of the depreciation laws? Well, guess what? It turns out that up until the year before, she was the receptionist. Yep. She went through the IRS training program and learned enough to be dangerous. I'm not putting her down. But her lack of experience could have cost my client $1,800 in taxes, penalties, and interest if he had gone instead of me. He may have been blind-sided and succumbed to her "authority."

If an auditor tells you the code says no to a certain big-ticket item deduction, ask for a written copy of the code section supporting his contention. Take the copy back to your tax pro to analyze.

The IRS shares its audit results with your state tax agency if you live in a state that levies income taxes. Usually within six months of receiving an audit determination from the IRS, you will get a letter from the state showing the same adjustments to income and deductions and billing you for the recalculated state income tax. It's rare that the state will also want to audit you. The states figure the IRS does a pretty thorough job and are happy to concur with its results. So there is usually no need to worry about getting hit again.

TAXPERTISE TIP

Don't sign the audit report unless it's a no-change or it results in a refund. The auditor will push to wrap it up right then and there. But if you are unhappy with the results, simply ask to take the report with you so you can discuss it with your tax pro. It might not seem like it, but there may be a light at the end of the tunnel. And if not, you can sign and send it back and wait for the bill.

Taxpertise Checklist

❑ Gather the information listed in the letter from the IRS.

❑ Check the totals of your receipts against the numbers listed on the tax return.

❑ Look for misstatements, omissions, or errors on the tax return.

❑ Look for missed deductions that can be used to reduce any increase in tax as a result of the audit.

❑ Review your strategy and discuss the audit with a tax pro.

We're In Real Trouble Now

Nonfilers

C'mon Down!

*C*andy bought a computer, rented an office space, and opened a residential relocation service. She hung up her sign and moved in. Business wasn't all that great in year one. It took a while for it to catch on. Luckily, Candy lived with her parents, who didn't charge her rent while she gave the business a go.

Candy enjoyed a modest $7,000 profit the first year. Certainly not enough to live on.

TAXPERTISE TIP

If you are self-employed, you should file a tax return even if, or I should say especially if, you have a loss. The loss can be carried back to prior years and net you a nice refund. If you have no tax liability in any of the recent prior years, you may carry forward the loss and subtract it from future income until it's used up. Either way, you're putting tax dollars back into your pocket.

"Do I have to file a tax return?" she asked.

"Well, yeah, why do you think you wouldn't have to?" I said.

"I hardly made any money, really," Candy said.

"If you're self-employed, you have to file if sales total $400 or more."

"What? Four hundred bucks and you got to file a tax return? I thought there was a window like you could make up to ten grand before you have to file."

I explained to Candy that the self-employment tax kicks in at $400 in sales.

Walt, one of the first clients I ever dealt with, showed losses on his business for the three years prior to my taking over the tax work. These losses could be carried back to prior years. Apparently, my predecessor did not understand that those losses meant money in Walt's pocket. I filed the appropriate forms and got him refunds of more than $3,000. Walt was a happy camper.

A couple of years ago Dave came to me. He hadn't filed taxes in 17 years. His new wife, Sue, insisted he get straight, so they hired me to handle the situation. Because Dave was self-employed, the tax bills would be higher due to the 15.3 percent self-employment tax that is added to the regular income tax. I cringed at the thought of what his tax bill might be.

The results were startling! Dave owed for only 2 years out of the 17. It turned out that if he had filed every year, he would have scored $35,000 in refunds from the IRS and another $17,000 in refunds from the state. Because he filed as head of household with a dependent child, making very little profit, he was entitled to the earned income tax credit, which translated to thousands of dollars in his pocket as a reward for working rather than being on welfare. He also had made estimated tax payments here and there over the years.

Did Dave get the refunds? No!

Refunds older than three years vanish. You can't even apply them to tax liabilities from other years.

But if you owe taxes, you must pay. The statute of limitations on collecting taxes is ten years from the date the IRS assesses the tax, which is normally right after you file the tax return. So if you file your 2000 income tax return in 2010, the collection statute does not run out until 2020. The clock begins ticking when the IRS finishes processing the tax return and assesses the taxes.

TAXPERTISE TIP

If you're self-employed and even if you don't think you have much to report, at least prepare the tax return. You may be surprised to see a refund (due to the earned income tax credit, or a loss that you can carry back).

In this particular case, Dave owed about $5,000 for a tax return that should have been filed 15 years ago. With penalties and interest, the amount had increased to $22,000.

I was able to convince the IRS to remove penalties for the tax years in which he owed. The IRS considers certain circumstances as "reasonable cause" to abate the penalties. Dave had gone through a horrible divorce, had been suicidal at one point, and was under a doctor's care for the duration. He had an ongoing prescription for anti-depressants. These factors weighed heavily in determining reasonable cause.

Penalties accrue at 5 percent per month for failure to file to a maximum of 25 percent of the tax liability. Failure to pay is .5 percent per month also to a maximum of 25 percent. You can accumulate almost half of your tax liability balance in penalties.

Although the IRS sometimes removes penalties, it refuses to abate the interest. It doesn't back off on the interest no matter how

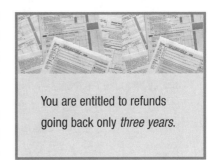

You are entitled to refunds going back only *three years*.

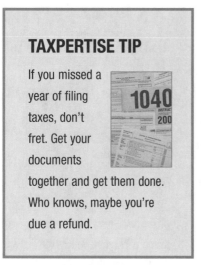

TAXPERTISE TIP

If you missed a year of filing taxes, don't fret. Get your documents together and get them done. Who knows, maybe you're due a refund.

hard you cry or how much you beg. The interest rate is changed quarterly and can run anywhere between 5 percent and 14 percent and upward, depending on the market rates.

Maybe like Dave, you are a groundhog who hasn't come up for air in quite some time. You fear the big, bad wolf is waiting topside with a shiny set of manacles. You don't know what to do. You haven't filed a tax return in ages, if ever, and you haven't heard a peep out of Uncle Sam. You fear the worst: jail time. You fear the second worst: an insurmountable tax liability that you will never be able to pay off in this lifetime.

Here's a little something to put your mind at ease: You are likely not a candidate for the orange suit and chain gang. In fact, the IRS will likely welcome you back like a prodigal son. Of course, it might spank you with some penalties.

"But what about all those people who end up in jail because of tax issues?" you ask. Well, check it out. It's always someone rich and famous—Wesley Snipes, Leona Helmsley, someone popular with the paparazzi, right? Makes for cheap publicity for the IRS to convey the message that you'd better file your tax return.

The IRS *could* throw you behind bars. The question is, will it? In my extensive experience, and in the experience of my colleagues, I find that the IRS is cooperative when dealing with nonfilers who are willing to cooperate, no matter how much they may owe or how many years they have failed to file.

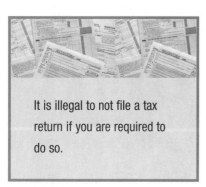

It is illegal to not file a tax return if you are required to do so.

Are you surprised? Well, the truth is, the IRS prefers to see you out there working and paying taxes. And that's pretty much a direct quote from a couple of IRS agents I've dealt with over the years. There is no benefit in flinging you behind bars, where you will be a burden to those who do pay their taxes. And if you're willing to seek forgiveness and promise to change your ways, they're willing to give you another chance.

Think positively. Look what happened with Dave.

If you haven't filed and haven't heard a word from the IRS, there's a possibility that the IRS owes you money. Just as in the story of Dave and Sue. He thought he'd owe a zillion bucks; he discussed that prospect with me, in fact. But look how that turned out. Every year the IRS talks about how much it owes individual taxpayers. The figure is always well into the millions and sometimes billions of dollars in unclaimed refunds because taxpayers do not file.

Another worrisome factor facing nonfilers is lack of paperwork from which to compile a tax return. Not such a big problem as you might think.

If you were self-employed, your bank and credit card companies can provide you with copies of statements and cancelled checks. If you don't have sales records, then in this particular case, the total of your bank deposits for the year will have to suffice. It would be important to know if any of the deposited funds were from other nontaxable sources, for example, transfers from personal accounts, loans, or gifts.

TAXPERTISE TIP

You can get a transcript of all of the third-party reporting documents the IRS and your state tax agency has on file—W-2s, 1099s, 1098s (mortgage interest statements), interest and dividend income, any other documents required for taxable and sometimes deductible transactions are available. Inquire about your payment history. You may find that like Dave, you made estimated tax payments or paid with an extension somewhere along the line. It doesn't matter how long ago you made these payments; you will get credit for them on the tax return.

From cancelled checks and credit card bills, reconstruct business expense deductions against your sales. Review the result to see if any figures look out of whack. If so, try to dig up more records or use a reasonable estimate.

If you can find your appointment book for the year in question, review it to jog a memory of other financial transactions. You may find clues to other deductible expenses. Or you may recall that you refinanced the house and deposited the funds to your business account. You wouldn't want to include this figure in sales. After all, loan proceeds are not taxable income.

Think about which vehicles you owned during the year in question. It would be advisable to create a mileage log for the vehicle expense deduction. If you have repair receipts for the vehicle, an odometer reading will be listed. Extrapolate your total mileage, then determine your business mileage from clues in your appointment book.

What business assets did you purchase? You may want to take advantage of the Section 179 deduction as well as standard depreciation.

In the absence of receipts, make a reasonable estimate of your expenses. And I mean Reasonable with a capital *R*. You don't want to traipse over the border of Reasonable into the area of Fraud. After all, part of your success with crawling out the hole you've been hiding in will be to do it with remorse and humility. So be very straightforward and honest, even if your tax liability will be horrendous. There are remedies for that situation as well.

You want to maintain credibility with the IRS at all times. Besides, if you are audited, undocumented deductions may be disallowed.

TAXPERTISE TIP

If you are filing more than one year of tax returns, do not mail them all in one envelope to the IRS. Don't ask me why, but the staff can't seem to figure out how to process more than one return at a time. Send each year's tax return separately with a separate check for payment. Put your Social Security number, the form number, and year on the memo line of the check to ensure that it is credited to the proper tax year.

But your chances of having them accepted will increase if you can demonstrate that your best guesses behind the expenses are necessary, ordinary, and reasonable.

If you are unable to pay, don't bother to include a letter. It will just get tossed; no one reads a letter included with a tax return. If you want to set up an installment plan, attach Form 9465 to the front of the most recent tax return. Fill out the form and be sure to include all tax years for which you owe. Then sit back and wait. It will likely take the IRS a couple of months to process the tax returns. You will eventually receive a letter approving or denying your request and instructions.

Getting back into the system is a wise course of action and more easily accomplished than you might think. The IRS is not waiting with handcuffs and whips, or a threat of debtors prison and financial ruin. It is made up of reasonable human beings who will work with you and your circumstances to resolve your tax issues. Won't it be nice to no longer look over your shoulder?

TAXPERTISE TIP

If you feel you have reasonable cause for abatement of penalties, wait for the bill that reflects the penalties and interest. Respond in writing, citing your reasons for not having filed or paid. Be sure to use the phrase "reasonable cause." Pay the tax but do not pay the penalty amount. Once the IRS has your money, it is more likely to keep it. If it denies your request, you can appeal or simply pay the bill.

Taxpertise Checklist

❑ File a tax return if you are self-employed with sales of $400 or more regardless of whether you have a tiny profit and especially if you have a loss.

❑ If you haven't filed for one year or more, remember it's against the law to not file if you are required to do so.

❑ If you have no records, use reasonable estimates. Try to get bank statements to reconstruct your financial history.

❑ Your appointment book will remind you of your financial transactions for the year and provide a basis for a mileage log.

❑ Expensive penalties may be abated for reasonable cause.

❑ Be honest, cooperative, and nice when reentering the system. Remember, you get more flies with honey and you'll stay out of jail!

Collections

Look Out! Here Come Roscoe and Vinnie

A new client named Maureen popped into my office one tax season. She told me, "I always did my own taxes because all I ever had was a W-2. Nothing fancy. But I quit my job and started a business last year and I'm not sure how to do the forms."

"Did you consult with a tax pro before you opened your business?"

"No. I know all the books tell you to do that, but I just didn't have the money for it. Besides, it's not like I opened some big, fancy corporation."

Great. Here's another one who loves big surprises. "Tell me about your business, Maureen."

Maureen had worked for years as a legal secretary making decent money. She stashed some away and used it to open a legal research firm. Since it was a service business, all she needed was a laptop and marketing materials. She wasn't rolling in the big bucks yet. And of course, she wanted to know how much she would owe in taxes. Her guess was she wouldn't owe anything because it "felt" like she was losing money.

I said, "I can give you a ballpark. Let's see your financial statements."

"Uh, here you go." A shoebox full of receipts and bank statements appeared on my desktop. Maureen's face had taken on a rosy hue.

OK . . . what could I say? I pulled out a ruler and measured the depth of the box. I maintained a straight face and said, "You can pretty much figure 300 bucks an inch. So it looks like you'll owe about 1,200 bucks in taxes."

Maureen's eyebrows disappeared into her hairline. Then she realized I was kidding.

Once the data was compiled, the bottom line showed a profit, which wasn't surprising. After all, it was a service-based business with minimal overhead, no substantial startup expenses, and no employees. Her sales totaled $40,000 but her expenses only came to about $20,000, leaving a taxable profit of $20,000. In California you can live a decent homeless lifestyle on that kind of money. But Maureen was one up on that scenario. She had survived on peanut butter sandwiches and a boyfriend who didn't charge rent.

When Maureen came back to pick up the tax return, I told her she owed $3,600.

"*What*???" the shriek could be heard for miles. Birds fell silent, keyboards quit clacking, and equipment stopped humming.

Maureen was up from her chair, pacing the room, stopping every few moments to wave her arms. "There's no way I can pay that! I don't have any money. You can see that from the tax return! I only made 20 grand! So how can I owe that much? Don't I get an exemption, a standard deduction? You can't even live on 20 grand. And they expect me to kick down almost $4,000? Have they no mercy? Don't they care about the little guy who's trying to open a business? And provide employment for other fellow Americans? Oh they'll bail out the banks and the automakers. What about me? Is this where my hard-earned money is going? I have to starve to death?"

Then she stopped pacing, slammed her palms onto the desktop, and narrowed her eyes. "I bet you made a big mistake, didn't you? Yeah, that's it. You screwed up the numbers somehow."

I got on the intercom to my receptionist, "Could someone get in here and swap out this coffee for decaf? Bring aspirin for two, and hurry, before she kills the messenger."

When Maureen settled down, I explained the bad news about the 15.3 percent self-employment tax. "You're right about the standard deduction and the exemption. That amount substantially reduces your taxable income. In fact, you don't owe much in income taxes at all, only about 600 bucks for the entire year. But see here?" I flipped to the Schedule C and Schedule SE and showed her the calculation for the self-employment tax, which represented the remaining $3,000 balance owed. "That funds your Social Security account. If you're self-employed, you are required to pay this amount."

INSTALLMENT AGREEMENTS

Once Maureen understood the rules, she sat back in her chair with a resigned and glum expression. "Well, whatever. The thing is, I can't pay it."

"Can you borrow the money? If you don't pay it by the April 15 deadline, the penalties and interest will be disastrous—worse than a loan shark. Plus, you really don't want to deal with the IRS if you don't have to."

Maureen shook her head. "I've maxed out my credit cards. Justin wants me to move out. He's tired of carrying me anyway. But that's not the hot issue. He's met someone else." A tear slid down her cheek.

Installment agreements are a good device when you have no other means to pay off the IRS.

Oh boy. I pushed the box of tissues toward her. "OK, let's set up an installment agreement with the IRS." I pulled out a Form 9465, a simple one-page request that provides the IRS with your basic information and the terms you can afford.

There is a user fee, which can be waived if your income is below a certain level. If you agree to direct debit of your monthly payments from your bank account, the user fee will be reduced.

You basically state how much you can pay each month and what day of the month you will make the payment. As long as you owe less than $25,000, can pay off the balance over a five-year period, and you don't owe taxes for any prior years, the IRS will more than likely accept your terms.

The Form 9465 can be filed with your tax return. Or you can go online to irs.gov. On the homepage is a pull-down menu on the top right titled "I Need To . . .". Select "Set Up a Payment Plan." Or you can find the form under "Forms and Publications," print it out, and mail it in.

As long as you keep up the payment arrangements, the IRS generally cannot levy your property. And it won't levy your property during the 30-day period in which it processes your agreement. It's a safe way to go when you owe.

Because the statute of limitations on collections is ten years, you can work out a deal over a longer period of time, if necessary. There's a lot more paperwork involved; it's a six-page form (Form 433-A and possibly Form 433-B) rather than a one-page form. You must disclose your finances in detail. The IRS will analyze your financial situation to determine your monthly payment. The IRS will file a lien, which will affect your credit report. Big hassle. Also very time-consuming. It would behoove you to budget a payment or get a loan or cash advance on a credit card to pay off the bill or at least part of it so that you can fulfill the obligation in five years or less.

If you've received some serious notices from the IRS, like "Intent to Levy," don't just mail the Form 9465 to the IRS. Call the phone number listed on the notice. A customer service rep will help you set up the installment plan and will make sure a hold is put on collection activity until it's processed. Get the employee's name and ID number. Make sure you document the date and content of your conversation.

Mail the payment 7 to 10 days before it is due because the IRS must receive the payment by the due date. It does not go by the postmark, as it would for honoring the due date for estimated tax payments or the due date for the tax return. The payment must not only be in hand but posted to your account by whatever date is indicated on the installment agreement.

In fact, this is a good reason to go with the auto debit from your checking account. The IRS will automatically debit your account on the due date. No remembering to mail the payment and no worries about the payment having arrived on time or getting lost in the mail. Another alternative is to set up an electronic account with the IRS and make your payments online.

If you find that you are unable to make one of the monthly payments, be sure to contact the IRS to let it know. During the course of the agreement, it will allow a couple of failures to pay without raising a fuss. But it's extremely important that you contact a service rep and request a one-month skip.

If you run into a few extra bucks and double up on payments during any given month, don't skip paying the following month's payment. The IRS does not treat a double payment as a payment in advance. In fact, it will likely send you a default notice and cancel the installment plan, which means more headaches and long phone hold times while attempting to reinstate the agreement.

COLLECTION ENFORCEMENT

In late 2006, the Internal Revenue Service announced the release of Roscoe and Vinnie, superenforcers who use extreme torture and extortion techniques to ensure collection of income tax liabilities. No one is safe. Even widows and small children will know who their daddy is.

OK, so it isn't that bad. But think about it. We have wars to finance, roads to build, an economy to save, and small third-world countries to support. One of the chief sources of all this financing is the income tax.

The current administration has calculated a tax gap of $300 billion. The tax gap represents the difference between what the IRS has collected and what is owed. This represents more than just uncollected liabilities reported on income tax returns; the IRS includes amounts it would be entitled to if everyone honestly reported his or her tax liabilities. We're talking about nonfilers, the underground cash economy, evaders, protestors, fudgers, and con artists, among others.

The IRS has substantially increased its collection and audit staff. Enforcement activity has been stepped up. The government is dead serious about collecting those old tax liabilities and performing more audits to create additional revenue.

And who falls behind in paying their tax debt most often? Entrepreneurs, that's who, and not necessarily because they aren't responsible. It's a matter of keeping up with those dang estimated tax payments.

When you're an employee, you're on the pay-as-you-go system. Taxes are deducted from every paycheck. As a sole proprietor or a partner in a partnership, there are no withholdings; you are required to make estimated tax payments on your projected profit. Oftentimes a self-employed individual makes just enough to take care of himself and his family. Without withholding requirements, estimated payments are often put on the back burner.

And it's not just income taxes that must be prepaid! Included in the estimated payment is 15.3 percent Social Security and Medicare tax based on your profit. Half, only 7.65 percent, is withheld from an employee's check. The boss picks up the tab for the other half of the employee's Social Security and Medicare. But now that you're the employee as well as the boss, you've got to shell out the full amount. And believe me, if you make a small profit, which most entrepreneurs are likely to do their first few years in business, you might have a hard time paying it.

If you owe back taxes, you may receive a letter stating, "Urgent!! We intend to levy on certain assets. Please respond NOW." That's enough to make a grown man cry. I know you picture waving bye-bye to your house, your car, and your firstborn. But there are steps you can take to prevent this action.

This letter has been passed from the shaking hands of a client into mine hundreds of times over the years. But not one of my clients has lost his assets, because they all took advantage of the many tools that protect taxpayers.

First of all, the IRS wants you out there working and paying taxes. It's not about to contribute to the homeless population simply because you are having problems and especially if you have been a law-abiding taxpayer for many years prior to your current crisis. The IRS can be cooperative when it comes to dealing with dire circumstances.

But if you're making enough to pay your taxes, and would rather party with the extra dollars instead, I encourage you to think twice. Tax liens look lousy on a credit report. And tax levies hitting your bank accounts or garnishments hitting your or your spouse's paychecks can send your finances into a tailspin.

PENALTIES

An IRS repayment plan is a lot more expensive than a loan shark's. Look at the penalties:

- Up to 25 percent for failure to file
- Up 25 percent for failure to pay
- As high as 100 percent for failure to pay payroll taxes (the trust fund portion)

And don't forget the interest on top of the penalties. You'd be wise to go on a credit card at 29 percent just to get rid of the IRS.

You may have reasonable cause to ask the IRS to abate the penalties against your tax liability. If you can convince it to do so, the amount you owe will be substantially reduced.

Another common penalty inflicted on the self-employed is the underpayment of estimated taxes penalty. If you don't pay, pay late, or underpay your estimated taxes, you will be subject to a penalty plus interest on the amount of taxes that should have been prepaid. The penalty is usually calculated when your tax pro prepares your tax return. Unless you look over the tax return carefully, you may not realize that you are paying a penalty in addition to your tax liability.

Check out your last tax return to see if there is a Form 2210 attached. The amount of the penalty will be listed on that form and transferred to the bottom of page 2 of the 1040 under the section titled "Amount You Owe, Estimated Tax Penalty."

Because the amount of the penalty and interest is driven by the payment due dates, you may receive a penalty notice for an additional amount due after the tax return has been processed.

Good news! You may have an out—if not for the full penalty, then at least for part of it. Here's how: Say, for example, the penalty occurs your first year of being self-employed. Perhaps you had a W-2 from your old employer for the first several months of the year. Then the last part of the year, while you were self-employed, you did okay but failed to make estimated tax payments.

Or let's say you had a lousy first half of the year. In fact, business was so bad, you considered closing it down. But you clung to your dreams, made it through, and had a favorable upturn in the last half of the year. And so you made no estimated tax payments until the final quarter or perhaps you made none at all.

In either situation, your bottom line and therefore your tax liability are all over the map. The IRS doesn't expect you to make an estimated tax payment if it appears you will owe nothing. That's why they are called estimates and that's why the amounts you are required to prepay are subject to change.

On Form 2210 there is a section in which you can annualize your taxable income to determine how much penalty, if any, applies to each quarter of the year. Instead of a flat-out

TAXPERTISE TIP

If you suspect you have underpaid your estimates, print out an annual  profit and loss statement displaying four columns for activity in each quarter. At the top of the report, hand-write, "Please annualize my income on Form 2210," and turn it over to your tax pro during your tax appointment. You may save yourself some money in penalties.

penalty, you can escape penalties for the quarters in which your liability would have been zero.

If you use QuickBooks, simply go to Reports, Company and Financial, Profit and Loss Standard. When the report comes up, change the dates to match your tax year. At the top of the report, click on Total By, select Quarter from the pull-down menu, and voilà, you'll have the quarterly report you need to determine your liability for estimated payments that quarter.

Other penalties aside from failure to file and failure to pay are negligence and fraud, which can be abated (made to go away) if you have a good reason. For example, if you experienced any of the following circumstances, you may be able to persuade an IRS agent to get rid of those expensive and pesky penalties:

■ Health problems
■ Depression
■ Alcoholism
■ Bad written tax advice from the IRS or a tax professional
■ A natural disaster that destroyed your records
■ A messy divorce
■ A tax professional who disappeared with your records
■ Any other reasonable cause for not filing or paying your taxes

When you receive a penalty notice, simply write a letter stating your circumstances. Then add the following: "I therefore believe I have reasonable cause and request that you abate the penalties." Include any backup documentation that helps prove your case (a prescription for Prozac, a letter from your doctor stating you are disabled, a recent unemployment compensation check stub, etc.).

If you are able, pay the base tax and the interest (the IRS will never abate interest), but do not pay the penalty amount. Once the IRS has your money, it is inclined to keep it.

Taxpertise Checklist

❑ Stay out of the IRS Collections Department. Borrow from a loan shark to pay off tax liabilities. It's cheaper and less of a headache.

❑ No one will lend you the money? Set up an installment agreement with the IRS by filing Form 9465.

❑ If you have "reasonable cause," request that the IRS abate penalties. The balance you owe will drop substantially.

Offers in Compromise

Step Right Up! Pay Pennies on the Dollar!

*I*f you have no money and no likelihood of ever having enough to pay your long overdue tax liabilities, don't worry. Be happy. Isn't that how the song goes?

Hey, at least you filed your tax returns. That's a big weight off your shoulders right there. I mean, you did read Chapter 20, about how it's against the law to not file tax returns if you're supposed to and how you could go to jail for it, right? If you've filed accurate tax returns, then you've got the get-out-of-jail-free card.

But you just don't have the money to pay the tax liability. In fact your prospects are so dim, you doubt you'd be able to resolve the debt within the ten-year statute of limitations.

Help is on the way! The IRS has a program called Offer in Compromise, which is designed to reduce your tax liability and forgive the overwhelming excess that would otherwise put you on the streets. Thanks to this program, many taxpayers are able to get a fresh start.

How can you qualify for an offer in compromise?

Maybe you owe a kazillion bucks (there are no debtors prisons in America). Making payments via an installment agreement won't put a dent in the liability; perhaps you can't even pay off the accumulating interest in this lifetime.

Or perhaps you are disabled or elderly or limited in some way that prevents the IRS from expecting repayment before the statute of limitations runs out.

Or there may be doubt as to liability. You filed a tax return and neglected to include some very large deductions. Or you received an erroneous tax document (1099, K-1, etc.) that the payer refused to correct and the statute of limitations for amending the tax return has passed.

If a situation like one of these applies to you, you also must currently be in compliance to qualify for an offer in compromise. You must have filed all tax returns and be making all required estimated tax payments. You must have at least a six-month payment history of estimated taxes for the current year.

UNCOLLECTABLE

Before you go for an offer in compromise, you should consider another route that is less complicated and less expensive. The IRS will not entertain an offer in compromise if your dire circumstances are only temporary. But you may obtain a temporary reprieve by being declared "uncollectable." Perhaps the balance owed isn't overwhelming, but because of unforeseen circumstances, you can't afford to make payments right now or in the near future. Perhaps you are unemployed or you are laid up and collecting temporary disability benefits but you anticipate being back to work in a year or two. If there is a light at the end of the tunnel, you may need only a short hiatus from the IRS.

The IRS will leave you alone while you struggle if it determines that you have insufficient funds to make monthly payments. Contact a service rep with your financial information. She will analyze your income and expenses and other resources to determine if she should in fact leave you alone.

Go to the IRS website and print out a copy of Form 433-A. It is six pages long. Do not fill in the entire form if you plan to speak to the IRS on the phone. Fill out page 6 first (self-employment information). Transfer the result to page 4 (Monthly Income/Expense Statement). After completing the statement on page 4, you will know if you can be deemed uncollectable. When you speak to an IRS agent on the phone, this is the information she will ask of you.

If you mail in a request to be considered uncollectable, you must complete all pages. I do not recommend submitting a written request. It takes longer and may get lost in the shuffle.

Let's get to work.

1. If you are self-employed, first provide your business income and expenses on page 6, section 6 of Form 433-A.

   a. Use the figures from last year's income tax return divided by 12 or use year-to-date data from the current year—the last quarter specifically—divided by 3. Because the income and expenses on page 4 are in monthly format, make sure that the self-employment income and expenses on page 6 coincide to monthly amounts.

   b. Move the resulting profit or loss to page 4, line 23, "Net Business Income."

2. Complete the remainder of page 4. Follow the instructions. List all other sources of income in the left-most columns, then complete the expense listings on the right. The first three items listed below must be pulled from tables on the IRS website; go to irs.gov. In the search engine, type in the capitalized titles in items a, b, and c

below. When the tables come up, select the amount(s) that apply to your situation.

a. *Groceries and Household Supplies.* Use the figure according to family size from National Standards—Food, Clothing, and Other Items on the IRS website.

b. *Housing and Utilities.* Use the lesser of your actual costs or the amount listed under National Standards—Housing and Utilities on the IRS website.

c. *Transportation.* Use the lesser of your actual costs or the figures from the National Standards Transportation table on the IRS website. Allowable expense is based on the number of vehicles and the region of the country you're in. List your ownership costs and operating costs; actual cost is limited by the max from the table. If your vehicle is used for both business and personal transportation, allocate the amount between page 4 and page 6 of Form 433-A.

d. List your actual monthly expenses for the remaining items in boxes 38 to 44. Be ready to back them up with receipts or other documentation.

e. List other expenses that are necessary to your and your dependents' welfare and survival or necessary to the production of income and attach a statement explaining their importance.

3. Subtract the total on line 45 from the total income on line 32. If the result is zero or less, you can be deemed uncollectable. If what remains is a positive number, you will be expected to pay that amount every month.

Either you or your tax pro can call the IRS Collections Department and provide the financial information over the telephone. The collection representative may argue with you about the validity of certain expenses or she may ask for substantiation of others. If it feels like it's going sideways, ask your tax pro to intervene.

In most cases, the IRS representative will refer the decision to the group manager. Collection activity will be suspended while the request is processed.

If you are declared uncollectable, the IRS will file a tax lien, which shows up on your credit report. But there will be no levies, no threatening letters, no Roscoe and Vinnie. Of course, interest and penalties will continue to accrue, and after so many years the amount you owe may escalate to an unbelievably high level.

AN OFFER IN COMPROMISE

You've seen it on television, heard it on radio: "Pay pennies on the dollar! Guaran-damn-teed!" Yeah, whatever. Do you get a bottle of snake oil with that?

A few folks have straggled into my office crestfallen about paying big fees to one of these so-called professionals, whom they never heard from again. Or if they did, it wasn't with the as-advertised "guaran-damn-teed" good results.

> **TAXPERTISE TIP**
>
> Hire a tax professional to review the form once you've completed pages 4 and 6 of Form 433-A. She will review your numbers and the formula. Her experience, knowledge, and insight will ensure that you have taken advantage of every allowable expense deduction and that you qualify to be declared uncollectable.

The good news is that offers in compromise are accepted quite often. I have helped clients get a fresh financial start by persuading the Internal Revenue Service to accept in settlement a dollar amount considerably lower than the tax liability owed.

Here are some examples:

■ A landscape designer suffering poor health settles a $28,000 tax bill for $1,032.

■ A machine shop owner who worked on his own offer in compromise for two years to settle a tax bill of $127,000 for $60,000 was turned down. I appealed and the IRS settled for $37,000.

■ A widower who owed $12,000 had no ability to repay. The IRS settled for $1,000.

- A self-employed midwife with a 28-year-old handicapped daughter who owed $103,000 settled for $3,200 and was able to pay it off on a one-year installment plan.
- An 81-year-old disabled woman on a poverty-level fixed income with no prospects of employment is now living in a storage locker and washing windows at the IRS building in Ogden, Utah, to pay off an $8,000 liability.

OK, OK, that last one is a lame joke. The point is that some offers, no matter how valid they might seem, just don't fly because the components don't shake out and the numbers don't crunch properly. The bad news is that not everyone qualifies for the deep discount.

You want to know the Big Secret to getting an accepted offer? The IRS uses a set formula to determine who will qualify for an offer in compromise and exactly how much it is willing to accept.

Here's the formula:

> Because the process is so intense and requires so much work and hand-holding, tax pros charge a small fortune to handle offers in compromise. So wouldn't you like to run your numbers through the IRS offer-in-compromise formula first before you spend the time, effort, stress level, and money with a professional who may or may not get the desired results?

$$\text{Total Equity in Assets} + (\text{Disposable Monthly Income} \times 48) = \$\text{Acceptable Offer}$$

If you must pay off an offer balance over time, use 60 rather than 48 in the above formula. This will increase the amount of the offer, but it will also give you more time to come up with what you owe.

It sounds a bit complex, but let me show you just how easy it is. After all, it's very simple math. It's the equivalent of 2 + 2. OK, there's a little subtraction and multiplication thrown in, but it really is not that tough to figure out. Let's take it step by step.

1. Completely fill in all six pages of Form 433-A.

2. Add up all the totals in Section 4, Personal Asset Information. This is the figure you will plug into the first variable of the formula, Total Equity in Assets.
3. Go to page 4. Take the figure on line 32, "Total Income," and subtract the figure on line 45, "Total Expenses." If the answer is a negative number, simply use zero. Otherwise, multiply the result by 48. This gives you the second component in the equation, Disposable Monthly Income x 48.
4. Add together the total from step 2 to the total from step 3 and this is roughly the amount that the IRS will probably accept to settle your tax bill.

I use the terms *roughly* and *probably* because the IRS will pick apart each component in the equation. I say "roughly" because the IRS's view of the value of your assets may be different than your view. And I say "probably" because the IRS agent will nitpick at every expense you list. Eventually, he may arrive at a different verdict than what you anticipated. Even so, it will likely not be too far off from the number you calculated when you tried the formula yourself.

Let's say you owe the IRS $35,000. You fill out the forms. In Section 4, Personal Asset Information, you list $1,000 in the bank, no investments, no available credit, no equity in anything. You rent an apartment; your car is financed up to its *Blue Book* value.

From page 4, Monthly Income/Expense Statement, after subtracting allowable monthly expenses from monthly income, your net is $100 per month multiplied by 48, which equals $4,800.

$1,000 (total assets) + $4,800 (net disposable income times 48) =
$5,800 (acceptable offer subject to bickering)

That's a big fat discount off $35,000, isn't it? You can't make a deal like that on a new car, not even with a trade-in. But like I said, it's subject to bickering. And here's the part that is time-consuming and stressful to the taxpayer:

- The IRS agent will do his own research to make sure you are disclosing all of your assets and to make sure you didn't recently transfer an asset to someone else's name, intending to hide it.

- He will argue over the validity of your expenses. He will look at copies of your bills with an eye toward justification of each expense.

- He will examine your bank statements to determine if you are reporting the correct amount of income and the correct average bank balance. If you list a bank balance of $20 on line 12C and the bank statements reveal an average balance of $3,000, guess which number he will add to the first variable, total equity in assets? Yep, three grand.

- If you have special circumstances, he will ask for more information to make a judgment on the validity of including the impact of those circumstances in his formula.

Let's break down these components. Total equity in assets is equivalent to the quick sale value of everything you own, essentially 80 percent of the hard assets you list. The value of your clothing and most household furnishings, jewelry, furs, artwork, your home, your car, and your business assets are valued at 80 percent of the listed equity. Equity is the difference between the value and any loan balances secured by the property.

Don't panic; the IRS is not asking for this information in order to grab your home or other assets and sell them. The IRS certainly doesn't want your furniture even if it would look better in its offices than those crappy metal desks. It doesn't work like that. It is merely putting numbers to your equity position for use in the formula.

Let's say your personal residence is worth less than the mortgage balance or you are

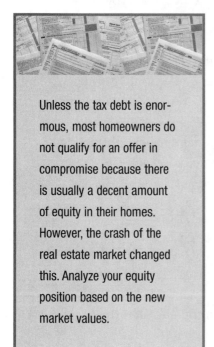

Unless the tax debt is enormous, most homeowners do not qualify for an offer in compromise because there is usually a decent amount of equity in their homes. However, the crash of the real estate market changed this. Analyze your equity position based on the new market values.

renting a modest apartment furnished by Ikea and driving a late-model car that's financed to the hilt. You don't have much of an equity position, do you? The car is probably worth the loan balance, if that, and the lien holder has priority. The only equity you have is sitting in your bank account and the available credit on charge cards that aren't maxed out. That's a good thing in terms of having an acceptable offer in compromise.

The next thing the IRS looks at is your disposable monthly income on page 4 of Form 433-A. This is computed by subtracting total allowable expenses (line 45) from your total monthly income (line 32). Your monthly income includes wages, disability payments, rents, net income from self-employment, and any other income from taxable or nontaxable sources.

On the IRS website, type "National Standards" into the search engine. You'll find a list of allowable expenses. Tables reflecting the maximum amount allowed for housing, utilities, groceries, and transportation are listed. Other allowable expenses include health insurance, medical bills, court-ordered payments, estimated income taxes, dependent care, and payments to a tax professional to get you out of this mess. Refer back to the "Uncollectable" section in this chapter for more information.

Allowable expenses do not include payments on credit cards or most other unsecured debt. The IRS figures those guys can get in line behind itself.

Although the formula is carved in stone, there are many factors that can be massaged into the calculations to change the value of each component in the formula. Anticipated increase or decline in income, health factors, and special needs of the taxpayer or her dependent(s) are a few of the factors that can turn the formula to your advantage.

The following are factors that weigh in to the taxpayer's advantage:

■ Advanced age
■ Medical conditions—physical or mental disabilities that hamper earning power
■ Special needs of dependents—disabilities or other factors that increase allowable expenses up to or beyond income potential

An experienced, honest, and empathetic tax professional can help you determine if there is flexibility in determining any of the values in the equation based on your particular circumstances. Excellent negotiation skills are a must. Knowledge of all the methods and rules, ins and outs, makes hiring a pro to handle your offer a worthwhile proposal.

If you are one of the lucky ones whose offer is accepted, make sure you stay in compliance with the tax laws. The IRS will keep an eye on you for five years. If you fail to make your estimated tax payments, pay any balance due, or file a tax return, it will rescind the offer and go after you for the original balance. It won't be very nice about it either. Some IRS agents seem to take it personally.

There's nothing more satisfying than seeing a deserving individual receive a fresh start. It's been a joy to help people with offers in compromise over the years. Financial disasters occur, situations get out of hand, and thankfully we have a government that can prove to be understanding and sometimes will give us a break.

Now that's some peace of mind.

Taxpertise Checklist

❑ Decide if you need a temporary break from tax collections (uncollectable) or a permanent solution (offer in compromise).

❑ Complete Form 433-A, page 6 and page 4, to see what the IRS will expect.

❑ Review your data with an experienced tax pro and discuss the proper resolution.

❑ Contact the IRS to have yourself deemed uncollectable, or submit an offer in compromise through a tax pro or by downloading Form 656 from the IRS website.

23

Innocent Spouse

Kill Him, Not Me!

I apologize in advance if this story sounds chauvinistic, but it is based on fact.

Belinda is a soccer mom with a fine husband and the prerequisite two kids. Ted, Belinda's husband, owns a hardware store that he put in Belinda's name so he could acquire business loans available only to women entrepreneurs.

Business thrives. Life is good. Ted works hard. Belinda bakes brownies, takes the kids to school, supervises the housekeeper, and works out with her personal trainer. (Are you ready to slap me yet?)

Ted brings home the income tax returns. "Sign here. And here," he says. Belinda doesn't know what it's all about and she doesn't rightly care because she's got the Range Rover, the credit cards, and the absolutely gorgeous, hardworking husband. So she signs here and here, then mixes up a pitcher of cosmos and goes on living her beautiful life.

One day Ted disappears along with all the money in the bank accounts. A few weeks later the police knock at Belinda's door and tell her the sad news. Ted's motorcycle went over a cliff off Highway 1. While the motorcycle was recovered, the body and the cash was not. It is presumed that he was thrown into the ocean.

And because there is no body, the life insurance company puts a hold on the funds it would normally pay to Belinda. Belinda is in dire straits. And the straits get even more dire when the State Board of Equalization shows up demanding a check for $100,000. Seems good old Ted didn't bother to remit sales taxes for five years.

Franchise Tax Board shows up next with an even bigger number to collect in unpaid state income taxes.

Not to be outdone, the IRS lands on all fours like Godzilla, shoots fire from its nostrils, and demands a catastrophic sum for payroll taxes and income taxes.

Belinda runs. She and the kids move in with Mom and Dad. She retreats into her old bedroom, plops onto her canopy bed, downs a six-pack (can't afford the cosmos anymore), and has a good cry. As she drinks and blubbers, she grows more and more suspicious about Ted's death. Why did he take every last dime out of the bank the day he died? And why did Brandy, his ever loyal secretary with the winning smile and hot little body, quit that same day, never to be heard from again? Where is Brandy anyway?

Belinda bolts upright. "Oh, hell no, he's not going to get away with this."

After Belinda sleeps off her hangover, she voices her suspicions to the police.

Well, sure enough, they find Ted and Brandy holed up in a love nest. Ted is sentenced to nine years for, among other charges, faking his own death.

Belinda tells her tale of woe to all of the tax collectors. Their response? "Gee, that's a shame, lady. But, uh, where's our money?" They still want to play hardball. After all, the liabilities are hers. The business is in her name and her name only. And even if it were in Ted's name only, half of that business would still belong to Belinda because they lived and worked in a community property state. She enjoyed the fruits of Ted's labor. And she signed the tax returns. This is adequate cause for the taxing agencies to hold her liable. But not just for half, for the entire sum. They are not going to let her off the hook.

TAX RELIEF FOR THE INNOCENT SPOUSE

Fortunately, there are steps that Belinda can take to resolve these liabilities. It falls under the claim of "innocent spouse tax relief." Belinda follows the steps and, with the help of a tax professional, is absolved of responsibility for all of the tax liabilities. She does not have to pay a red cent.

If your story is similar, you too may be entitled to relief from the tax debt incurred by your spouse. And if your story is equally dramatic, or possibly more so, perhaps you'll simply want to sell it to Lifetime as the next movie of the week and use the proceeds to pay off the tax bills.

Filing an innocent spouse claim is a difficult and time-consuming process, especially in a community property state. For starters, check out the following excerpt from the IRS website to see if you qualify for innocent spouse tax relief:

> **TAXPERTISE TIP**
>
> I urge you to seek help from a professional who has experience and success in representing taxpayers for issues relating to an innocent spouse claim.

1. The taxes owed are your spouse's or ex-spouse's.
2. You are no longer married to that spouse.
3. You thought your spouse would pay the taxes on the original return.

4. If there was an audit of the tax return, you didn't know about the items changed in the audit that resulted in a new tax liability.

5. You would suffer a financial hardship if you were required to pay the tax. You would not be able to pay for basic living expenses like food, shelter, and clothing.

6. You did not significantly benefit (above normal support) from the unpaid taxes.

7. You suffered abuse during your marriage.

Do you believe that your situation meets the above requirements? If so, download Publication 971 from the IRS website and study it. If you qualify for equitable relief, file IRS Form 8857. You must file this form no later than two years from the date the IRS first attempted to collect the tax from you.

Divorce doesn't solve your tax problems. If you and your spouse are divorced, do not assume that you are no longer liable even if the divorce decree states that your ex-spouse is responsible for all the taxes including prior-year liabilities. The Internal Revenue Service doesn't care what the divorce decree says; you signed the tax return and you are liable. The divorce decree certainly gives you the right to go after your ex and sue the hell out of him, but that's up to you. The IRS will still garnish your wages or put a lien on your house or yank money out of your bank account. Or, and here's the most common occurrence, take your tax refund and apply it to any prior-year liabilities your ex promised to pay. Ouch! That will leave a mark. That concept is known as "injured spouse."

As an aside, you should know that the same attitude applies for determining who can claim the children as dependents. If the divorce decree states that you get the deduction for the kids, but your spouse files first and takes them as dependents, the IRS will honor your spouse's claim. The IRS doesn't know what your divorce decree says, and she doesn't care. She will get involved if you complain and prove to the IRS that you provided more than 50 percent of the kids' support and prove that they lived with you for more than half of the year. Those two factors alone overrule any divorce decree saying otherwise.

Perhaps you, the innocent spouse, married someone with existing tax problems that you had nothing to do with. You came into the marriage with some assets of your own: a retirement plan or an unencumbered rental property left to you by Uncle Henry. The IRS may want to tap into those assets to satisfy your spouse's old tax bill. "Unfair!" you cry. "Why should I pay when it was my spouse who messed up?"

Let's say you know your spouse is a bum when it comes to taxes and you decide early on to play it smart. That's what Jenny did. Fifteen years ago, she married Kevin, who owns a carpet-cleaning business. It was a second marriage for the both of them. Jenny sold her house and took the proceeds to use as a down payment on a new home for her and Kevin.

Kevin had no money to contribute because he didn't own property. Jenny didn't care. She loved the man and wanted to share. The lovebirds were blissfully happy. But Jenny noticed that Kevin, despite having what appeared to be a moderately successful, in-demand business, always seemed to have financial problems.

Jenny had her own demanding career and didn't know much about Kevin's business affairs. One day, however, she answered the door to find Scottie, one of Kevin's employees. "I need a W-2 this year," he said. "My wife and I are trying to buy a house."

Jenny drew back. "What? This year? Don't you always get a W-2?"

Scottie shrugged and gave her a lopsided grin. "Nah. We all kind of work under the table."

"Under the table? What the hell?"

When the shock wore off, Jenny ransacked Kevin's office. No payroll records anywhere. She grabbed up their jointly filed tax return and paid a visit to Jack, the accountant who had prepared it.

Jack said that he had told Kevin to put his workers on payroll, but Kevin had ignored the advice. He'd continued to pay his workers without withholding taxes. The expense was recorded on his business Schedule C under subcontract labor. "Completely inappropriate," Jack said. "If the IRS or the state were to come in for an audit, they would reclassify those payments as payroll and Kevin would be presented with a huge payroll tax bill. Not only that, but he doesn't even give the workers 1099s. He should at least do that. And it's likely he's not getting the full deduction because half the time he pays the guys cash."

Jenny absorbed this and then with a note of panic in her voice, she asked, "So does that mean he hasn't been paying workers' compensation insurance either?"

"That's right."

"So if someone gets hurt on the job, they could sue us and we could lose the house, lose everything?"

"I'm not a lawyer, but I'd have to say right again."

After a few muttered expletives, and a blood pressure check, Jenny continued. "Something else I've been meaning to ask. The taxes we owed seemed pretty high. Why is that? When I was single, I usually got a refund."

Jack leaned forward and clasped his hands together. "Kevin never makes his estimated tax payments."

"What? So I'm picking up the tab on his liability? And here I thought it was because of that so-called marriage penalty. Why wasn't I told about this?"

Jack shrugged and busied himself flipping a pencil.

"Is there anything else I should know?"

"Yep," Jack said. "Kevin owes taxes for every year since he started the business five years ago. He didn't tell you?"

Dazed, Jenny mumbled, "He said something about tax issues but said you were handling it."

Derisive snort. "I set him up on an installment agreement, but he defaulted."

"And now? What's going on now?"

Jack shrugged. "I don't know. I haven't heard anything. But I'm sure the shoe is ready to drop."

Three months later, Jenny and Kevin were still married, perhaps not as blissfully. Jenny loved the guy and would never leave him, but she had already raised three kids, thank you very much, and was not willing to raise a fourth. When she came to see me, she had, with the help of an attorney, already made some wise moves:

- Kevin had signed a quitclaim deed to the house, making Jenny the sole owner. Kevin's name was also removed from the mortgage loan. "It's my house. I put the money into the house, have made all the house payments, and damn it, I'm not about to lose it over Kevin's financial issues," Jenny said.

- Kevin had signed a rental agreement and begun making monthly rent payments to Jenny. The rent was calculated at fair market value and included utilities.

- Jenny had put the utility bills in her name only.

- Jenny had closed the joint checking account and opened one in her name only, where she deposited Kevin's rent payment and her paycheck.

- Jenny and Kevin now maintained their finances separately. No funds were commingled; no purchases were made jointly, including cars, boats, and furniture.

- Jenny had removed herself as co-owner of Kevin's business. She'd also removed her name as signing authority on Kevin's business checking account.

- Jenny had prepared her tax return claiming the status of married, filing separately.

By following these procedures, Jenny protected her assets. Over the years, she nervously watched as her husband avoided his tax issues.

Protect your assets and protect your income. If it was your money that paid for the house the two of you live in, you shouldn't have to worry about tax liens against it because your spouse is messing up. If you have a wonderful career, you certainly don't want to experience the loss of your wages to garnishment, much less suffer that humiliation. And you don't want to be at the checkout line at the grocery store when your debit card is rejected because your bank account has been levied.

If you play it smart the way Jenny did, you still may not be safe from the clutches of our taxing agencies, especially if you live in a community property state, where what is his is yours and vice versa. The IRS will claim that applies to tax liabilities as well. The key however, is to prove that you received no benefit from the income earned by the delinquent spouse. More importantly, take preventive action by financially separating yourself from your dangerous spouse.

Taxpertise Checklist

❑ File a separate tax return from your spouse. The filing status of married, filing separately is generally more expensive but may overall be worthwhile.

❑ Keep your money and business affairs separate. No joint checking accounts, no joint ownership of any assets. Treat your spouse like a roommate (with benefits). If you own the house, then your spouse should sign a rental agreement and pay rent and his fair share of household expenses on a monthly basis.

❑ If your spouse is self-employed, do not become a part of the business. Don't be on payroll, don't be a signer on the business bank accounts, don't co-sign loans, don't be a corporate officer or shareholder.

Financial Wellness

Que Sera, Sera

A friend recently asked, "What is the best business to be in to make lots of money?" The answer, as demonstrated by the following story, is "It doesn't matter."

John and Fred are both self-employed electricians. They each started from nothing. Both learned the trade, took the electrical contractor's exam, and set up their own individual shops. This is where the similarities end; each story tromps down a different path.

After 20 years, John has a hundred grand in his business checking account, a retirement plan, a brand-new truck, a time share in Cabo, and several rental properties. He's 50 years old and is set to retire in five years.

Fred is overdrawn in his business checking account, is renting a room in his girlfriend's house, and is driving a beater. He has no retirement plan, no vacations, no investments whatsoever. All he has are fear and stress.

Given the same opportunities, talents, and financial starts, John ended up at the rainbow's end while Fred is drowning in the La Brea Tar Pits of Financial Despair. They ended at opposite ends of the spectrum. What happened?

Let's talk about fear and stress for a moment. Now, I'm not a psychotherapist, a marriage counselor, or a doctor of any sort. I took Psych 101 in college and recall something about Pavlov's dogs, which always makes me think of how the government implements tax law in order to convince us to behave economically in a certain fashion, but I'll save that for the funny papers.

Back to fear and stress. Many people suffer fear and stress around the topic of money. Money, the root of all evil, was responsible for investors leaping to their deaths from Wall Street windows in 1929. It breaks up marriages, causes insomnia, and destroys business and personal friendships.

And for those with tax problems, fear and stress are compounded. Individuals who have not filed tax returns for many years are looking over their shoulders. Taxpayers who have filed but haven't paid lie awake in worry. Taxpayers who fudged wonder if they will get caught and go to jail. No matter what the tax problem, most folks would like to come clean, but they fear

- being arrested,
- increasing debt without ability to repay,
- losing assets, and
- humiliation in the eyes of family and friends.

According to modern science, much of the physical illness folks suffer can be traced to fear and stress. And much of our fear and stress can be traced to financial problems, including tax problems.

Becoming financially healthy involves more than changing spending habits, learning how to budget, and saving for retirement. In fact, all of those dos are difficult to achieve. Attaining financial health becomes a major project and involves changing who you are. Is that possible? Unlikely, at least for the long run. If nothing else, it's a lot of work to accomplish these changes. Some people don't even know where to start or what to do to achieve a financial goal even if it's a small goal, like becoming better organized.

But one accomplishment that will be the root to all this change is not so difficult if your mind is open to accepting a new perspective: loss of fear.

My most primal fear is falling into bad health. If I get a headache, it must mean a brain tumor has formed. If my foot falls asleep, am I having a stroke? I check the mirror to see if my smile is intact; I raise my arms.

I notice, however, that I have no fears when it comes to money. If I'm flat broke, I shrug and say, "I'm flat broke." Money comes and money goes, but it cannot kill me. It cannot kill me like this splinter in my finger. The one that I just know is not really a splinter, but a bite from a flesh-eating recluse spider. I fear a horrible death awaits me.

Somewhere along the line, I got tired of thinking these thoughts, tired of living in fear, especially when the headache turned out to be just that and not a malignant brain tumor, when the rapid heartbeat wasn't the beginning of a heart attack but merely an emotional disturbance. And somewhere along the line, I noticed that clients and friends who were experiencing financial difficulties treated these difficulties with the same sense of fear and foreboding with which I treated my every potential physical health symptom.

I would try to cheer them up (accompanied by a mental eye roll) much the same way they would try to cheer me up with a glass of water and some aspirin and a bit of playful admonition.

And so one day, I said to myself, "That's it." If I get a headache, it's just a headache. If it turns worse (after all, we all must die one day), then that will be my lot, but I will not live in fear because this fear and stress will cause illness and an early demise. Every once in a while, I have to remind myself. But hey, my attitude has improved considerably.

Think of what you do not fear but notice that others fear. Do you know someone who is scared to roller-skate or ride a bike and you aren't? Or if you're not afraid of flying, do you know others who are? And what do you think of their fear as compared with your lack of fear in that area? Don't you pretty much come to the conclusion of "Hey, if the plane is going to crash, it's going to crash. C'est la vie. Que sera, sera, and all that, right?" Now try to look at your finances and tax fears in the same light. Que sera, sera.

Once you realize that you will live, you will survive, even if you are flat-ass broke, then you can begin to face your financial dilemmas and relax. Once you are relaxed, you will have the clear head you need in order to correct your situation. If you are not scared of the IRS, you will be able to step forward and fix the fine mess you got yourself into. And once that mess is straightened up, then you can exhale, quit looking over your shoulder, and get on with your life.

Aside from losing the fear, you must discover that the problems you have are not insurmountable. In fact, there are some wonderful solutions. Let's look back at those four expressions of fear and let me give you some insight into dispelling them:

- *Being arrested.* Don't worry! The IRS wants you out there working, in the system, in compliance, and paying your share. It is extremely rare for the IRS to arrest a taxpayer. In 25 years, I have yet to see a nonfiler or someone who cheated on his taxes go to jail for the crime. I'm not saying it doesn't happen, but it's highly unlikely. If a person is jailed, chances are he was completely uncooperative and angered the monster.
- *Increasing tax debt without ability to repay.* If you find yourself in this situation, many tools are available to help you:
  - Installment agreements

- Offers in compromise to reduce the liability to an amount you can afford
- Being deemed uncollectable due to financial hardship, in which case collection efforts cease until you are able to pay
- Abatement of stiff penalties for reasonable cause—alcoholism, depression, a bad divorce, bad tax advice, a natural disaster that destroyed records, etc.

■ *Losing assets.* This will happen only if you ignore the situation for too long. Even then, there are methods to retrieve said assets. The trick is to face your situation head-on. If you cooperate with our taxing agencies, they will cooperate with you.

■ *Scorn from family and friends.* Hey, if they don't know that you flaked on your taxes, why tell them now? The IRS won't tell them. If the IRS files a tax lien, it will show up on your credit report, just like any other lien, judgment, or bankruptcy. But if anyone calls the IRS (as if anyone would)—individuals, lenders, bankers—the IRS will not respond to the queries because your tax account is confidential.

Still having trouble? Seek out a counselor who is qualified to help alleviate your fears. You may also ask for help from an organizer, a professional financial planner, your tax pro, or even a friend or relative who seems to have it together when it comes to finances. You can find a solution to your dilemma if you look hard enough and put in the time and effort required to resolve it.

■   ■   ■

AFTERWORD

I think of the United States as a big, wonderful club to which we belong. When we pay our taxes, we are paying dues to be members of this club. And we are reaping the benefits. The highways we drive upon, the libraries we visit, the schools our children attend, and many other goods and services are provided thanks to the many Americans who voluntarily pay their fair share.

Approximately one-third of our less fortunate citizens pay no taxes whatsoever. And with the current administration this figure may rise to as much as 50 percent. In fact, because of the earned income tax credit, these folks enjoy a reverse welfare system. Rather than paying their dues, they are paid thousands of dollars for being in the club. By the same token, many giant corporations work the tax system to substantially reduce payment of their fair share. And they get their own earned income tax credit in the form of economic bailouts. Other folks dodge the IRS by not filing, not paying, or both. Looks like it's the guys in the middle that need the bigger shoulders. The tax system was not meant to serve as a means to redistribute wealth. Yet, this appears to have happened.

I suspect, dear reader, that you are one of the ones in the middle with the big shoulders. I encourage you to not be discouraged. Comply with the laws of this great nation and continue to pay your fair share. Lobby for change, make your voice heard, and in the meantime, have no fear.

Appendices

Records Retention

How Long Do I Have to Keep This Stuff?

*T*he only reason you keep any paperwork is because you

- *need proof of purchase to get a refund on a product gone bad,*
- *might get audited, or*
- *suffer from disposophobia—you pack rat, you!*

Let's look at what the IRS recommends in Publication 583. First, it says you should keep tax returns for three years, but hold up! You'd better keep them longer than that because most states have an additional year to go after you. If your state gets wind of changes from an IRS audit, it will bill you accordingly. It may also want to audit you (but it's doubtful). Almost every records retention expert out there will tell you to keep your tax returns permanently. The main reason for this is that some items and carry-forwards (capital losses, net operating losses, unused credits, etc.) on the tax return can affect current and future years. So it is a good idea to have on hand the tax return for the year in which the carry-forward originated in order to prove your case.

If you amend an income tax return, the statute of limitations is extended, so hang onto everything for an extra three to four years after you amend the tax return.

You're going to love this one: If you have tax returns in which you have understated your gross income by 25 percent, keep them for six years. Got a little minor fraud going? Keep those tax returns!

Even better: a full-blown fraudulent income tax return should be kept indefinitely. That's right; it's listed right there in the IRS publication. If you write really good fiction, don't throw it away. Maybe they want to give you an Oscar.

If you file a claim for a loss from a worthless security or a bad debt deduction, you should keep the documentation and the tax return for seven years.

In terms of your books and records, you should keep all backup documentation to prove your case to the IRS for as long as the audit period is open.

- If you haven't filed a tax return for the year in question, the audit period will be open until three to four (state) years after you file. So keep those records at least until then.
- If a certain transaction creates a carry-forward, keep the records until the audit period expires once the carry-forward is used up. For example, you sell some stock for a capital loss of $100,000. The IRS allows you to apply this loss to other capital gains. But say you suck at stock market transactions and have no capital gains. You can take only $3,000 of this loss each year until it's used up. OK, 33

years have gone by and you're being audited. The auditor says, "What the hell is this capital loss carry-forward?" You'd better be able to pull out the original paperwork to prove that you had the capital loss; otherwise you might have an argument on your hands.

■ Payroll records (from the original employment application to time sheets, to payroll tax returns, etc.) should be kept for seven years. The IRS requires you to keep the records for four years; the U.S. Department of Labor wants them kept for three years. But your attorney will want you to keep them for seven years.

About the Author

*B*onnie Lee is an Enrolled Agent admitted to practice representing taxpayers in all 50 states at all levels within the Internal Revenue Service. Bonnie Lee founded Symmetry Business Services to represent taxpayers in audits, offers in compromise, and tax problem resolution as well as to help nonfilers safely reenter the system. For more than two decades, she has specialized in issues relating to independent contractors, self-employed individuals, and real estate professionals. As an outgrowth of her work with clients, her practice now includes financial wellness and prosperity coaching, enabling people to be the best they can be, which is the main subject of her Taxpertise seminar program.

After 25 years of going to bat for her clients—dealing with auditors, specialists, problem resolution officers, tax advocates, and liaison personnel—she has an excellent take on what works and what doesn't. She knows what goes on within the walls at the Internal Revenue Service. She knows the secret handshakes. She has the decoder ring. She will show you how to cut through the red tape and cut to the chase to solve tax problems. From managing a full-scale office audit bordering on criminal charges, to greatly reducing huge tax liabilities through offers in compromise, to resolving innocent spouse problems, to correcting IRS errors, you name it, she's dealt with it! And for the most part, her clients come out grinning from ear to ear.

A native of San Francisco, Bonnie currently resides in Sonoma, California, with her little dog, Harley.

Glossary

Abate. Reduction or elimination of an assessment—usually a penalty by the IRS.

Amortization. Writing off the cost of an intangible asset (goodwill, covenant not to compete, points, etc.) over its useful life.

Assess. Establishing the legal liability of the tax due after processing a tax return.

Audit. The investigation of a taxpayer's tax returns to verify accuracy.

Basis of property. A monetary designation of a taxpayer's investment in a property, usually cost.

CPA—Certified Public Accountant. A tax professional licensed by the state.

Credit. An amount that directly offsets a tax liability, versus a deduction which reduces taxable income.

Deduction. An amount subtracted from taxable income.

Depreciation. Writing off the cost of capital assets over their useful lives.

Dividends. A distribution of money or property other than stock or the right to purchase stock from a corporation to its shareholders.

Double taxation. The characteristic of imposing two taxes on one C corporate profit—once at the corporate level when dividends, which are not deductible, are paid and then at the shareholder's individual level when he must pay tax on dividends received.

Enrolled agent. A tax professional licensed at the federal level who may represent taxpayers at all levels within the Internal Revenue Service.

Estimated taxes. In the absence of adequate paycheck withholding, income taxes paid in advance of year-end on the basis of anticipated tax liabilities, generally from self-employment activities.

Exclusive use. Designation of an asset's depreciable basis to 100 percent business when there is no personal use to allocate.

Hobby loss. Reclassification of a self-employment venture that is not treated as a business. Hobby losses are not deductible on a tax return. Hobby income can be decreased but not beyond zero by allowable deductions.

Injured spouse. A spouse who loses income tax refunds because of obligations incurred by usually an ex-spouse.

Innocent spouse. A spouse who did not significantly benefit from erroneous omissions on a joint income tax return, or who is otherwise exempt under an exception to the general rule of joint and several liability on a joint income tax return.

Intent. A concept on which the deductibility of certain business expenses hinges.

Lavish and extravagant. A criteria used when determining the deductibility of meals and entertainment expenses.

Levy. A power granted to the IRS to seize and sell the property of a taxpayer to satisfy a tax debt.

Lien. A claim that attaches to or encumbers property owned by a taxpayer as collateral for a tax debt.

No-change audit. The result of an audit in which no adjustments are made to your income tax return and therefore no money is owed to the taxing authority. This inspires confidence that you know the rules and act accordingly and will stop auditors from examining other years.

Offer in compromise. A process available to possibly reduce tax liabilities based on hardship. Forms 433-A and 656 must be completed.

Ordinary and necessary. A concept used to judge the validity of a business tax deduction.

Principal place of business. Used in conjunction with home office; a requirement that the home office be the taxpayer's principal place of business.

Reasonable cause. A term to use when corresponding or speaking with the IRS to justify not having filed or paid tax liabilities. Reasonable cause includes bad tax advice, loss of records due to a natural disaster, mental and physical health problems, and so on.

Reasonable compensation. Used in conjunction with S corporations to ensure that principals of the corporation are taking an acceptable amount of compensation in the form of payroll.

Related party transactions. Refers to taxable transactions between individuals related by blood or between individuals and business entities in which they maintain a controlling interest.

Self-employment tax. A tax of 15.3 percent of profit levied on self-employed individuals to fund her Social Security and Medicare accounts.

Trust account. Taxes owed to the government that are entrusted to a business owner. Sales tax and payroll tax withholdings are two common examples of trust account taxes. Neglecting to pass them to the government by the due date results in substantially higher penalties than other tax delinquencies.

Uncollectable. (Also known as Section 53.) Based upon an IRS formula, you can be deemed uncollectable and relieved from payment of unpaid tax liabilities for a period of one year. While no collection efforts will be made, the balance will continue to accrue penalties and interest.

Index

TAXPERTISE

TAXPERTISE